EMILY GOSSE

To my own dear

JEN

EMILY GOSSE:

A LIFE OF FAITH AND WORKS

The story of her life and witness
with her published poems and
samples of her prose writings.

by

ROBERT BOYD

Published by Olivet Books
Copyright © Robert Boyd 2004

ISBN 0-9548283-0-5

36 Clachnaharry Court
Clachnaharry Road
Inverness
IV3 8LT

Printed and Bound in Great Britain by CPI Bath Press, Bath

EMILY GOSSE (née BOWES)

CONTENTS

Foreword by Dr S S Short

My knowledge of and close friendship with Robert Boyd extends to well over half a century, and one of the greatest joys of my life has been to pay an annual visit, (lasting a few days), to the home of his dear wife Jen, while she was still with us and himself in Fort William in the Western Highlands of Scotland.

I have long been aware of the great interest which Robert took in the highly renowned Gosse family, and I was greatly struck by the meticulous research which he made with regard to the detail of their lives. About Philip Gosse, F.R.S., and his son Edmund, others have researched and written, (though I question whether their researches have been as thorough as those of Robert); but about Philip's first wife Emily, and the mother of Edmund, much less has appeared in print. And yet she was a lady with outstanding talents.

During recent years, when staying in Robert's home, I have read something of her life and have perused much of her poetry, and this has left a tremendous impression on me. What a pity it would be, I have often felt, if these delightful poems were allowed to pass, through neglect, away into oblivion! Her versification of the story of Abraham's temptation and the 22nd Psalm are, in my opinion, works of genius; and so are many of her other compositions.

My prayer is that this presentation of the story of her life and the record of some of her writings may prove, through the Holy Spirit, a rich blessing to all who have the privilege of reading this book.

Stephen S. Short

Weston-super-Mare

Preface

Many years ago I was given a copy of Anna Shipton's *Tell Jesus: Recollections of Emily Gosse.* In reading it I was greatly impressed with the deep sincerity and transparent devoutness of its subject. Quite a number of years later I read *Father and Son* by Edmund Gosse, but I did not immediately realise that Mrs Shipton's Emily was Edmund's mother. When I did, I felt compelled to explore further by reading the same author's *Life of Philip Gosse, FRS* (1890), and so there began years of investigation in the course of which I uncovered much that had not been told by Edmund, some of which was apparently unknown to him.

One memorable day was the 1st November, 1966, when the foreman at Abney Park Cemetery, Stoke Newington in London, conducted me to grave no.17673 where Emily was buried. The headstone had weathered but was clearly legible more than a hundred years after its erection. The grave looked neglected, but still standing nearby was the ancient elm tree mentioned by Anna Shipton in, *Tell Jesus,* its trunk having grown to more than three feet in diameter when I saw it.

Another landmark in these researches of mine was when, on one of my visits to 58 Huntingdon Street in Barnsbury, Emily and her husband's last home together, I noticed that the house next door was being completely renovated by contractors. As the houses in the terrace were identical, it was touching to go from room to room of the three stories of the latter, and up to its attic and down to its basement. It was thus easy for me to picture the Gosse household in occupation next door, looking out of its front windows to the street, or from its back windows to the garden which extended about thirty feet from the house. I could also see for myself the dimensions of the rooms and passage-ways and their layout.

So began a series of visits to all (or most) places connected with Emily Gosse each contributing to the picture of her life and times from her childhood in Merionethshire and her governess post in Berkshire to her

London residences in Upper Clapton, De Beauvoir Square, and lastly Huntingdon Street.

About the same period I met Douglas Wertheimer who was research-ing his doctoral thesis for Toronto University, and Richard Freeman of University College, London, who had gathered a large collection of the writings of P H Gosse. These contacts were valuable to all three of us as we were able to exchange information gleaned in our respective researches, and to correspond on points of mutual interest.

The opportunity has been taken of reproducing here a few samples of Emily's Gospel tracts and some of the articles she had subscribed to vari-ous periodicals. At the same time, having shown several of her poems to friends who greatly admired them, I have decided to include all her known poems so that they may delight a new generation.

To Miss Jennifer Gosse, Emily's great-granddaughter, I wish to ac-knowledge a debt of gratitude for her helpfulness in making the material of the Gosse family collection available to me, as I do for that given by the many staff members of libraries, record offices, etc, too numerous to list here. Special thanks are due to Mr Michael Ritchie for his general en-couragement and help in making this work presentable, to Howard Coles for help in preparing Emily's poems for publication, to Dr Stephen Short for his enthusiastic interest and for contributing the generous foreword, and lastly, and most especially, to my dear wife to whose memory this lit-tle volume is dedicated; she shared my interest, accompanied me in my visits, and so gladly and competently executed a considerable amount of typing on my behalf.

May the unfolding by me in this book of the life of one who laboured so diligently for and continued to cling in faith so closely to the Saviour even in her most intense suffering, draw my readers to love and serve the Saviour too with like unswerving faith.

ROBERT BOYD

▌Introduction

The Gosses of London and south Devon are known today largely through two books, *Omphalos,* by P H Gosse, and *Father and Son,* by Edmund Gosse. In the former, Philip Gosse set out his *attempt to untie the geological knot* by submitting that all organic nature moves in a cycle, and creation, having to commence somewhere, is an irruption into the cycle. It was published in November, 1857 and has never been reprinted since. By contrast, what Edmund called his "study of two temperaments" was first published in 1907 and has gone through many editions from then until the present day. In the last forty years, however, thanks to access to original correspondence and diaries, more has become known about the two authors, and earlier impressions have been corrected in several areas. Mention should be made of: *Gosse: the life of Philip Gosse,* by L R Croft, Preston, 2000, and *Glimpses of the Wonderful; the Life of P H Gosse,* by Ann Thwaite, London, 2002.

The subject of the present work is Emily, the wife of P H Gosse and the mother of Edmund. This study of her fifty years is a study of the development of a faith which, because of being subjected to exacting tests of it, emerged to be admired by her friends and by many readers of Anna Shipton's devotional writings. Edmund, who was only seven years old when his mother died, has shown in his sparse references to her that this rich faith of hers was little recognised by him. It is the present author's conviction that Edmund Gosse's failure to appreciate his mother's faith deprived his readers of an accurate picture of this remarkable lady.

The first half of the nineteenth century was a period of considerable development in England. The London in which Emily Bowes was born in 1806 was to be radically transformed by industrialisation, by the construction of railways, by immigration particularly from Eastern Europe, and by building out around the city's neighbouring towns and villages, so turning them into London suburbs. During that half-century the religious scene was being transformed too. The rise in the influence of the evangelical movement in the Church of England was soon to be followed by that of the Tractarian movement and by the growth of non-conformist bodies. After living for thirty-four years mainly in rural parts of the country, Emily's last years were spent in this new London where her faith blossomed right up to and throughout her closing years.

The present study is an attempt to examine the influences of environment, parental training, friendships and appropriate literature, etc, on the development of the character of the young mother who was to be so tragically taken from her family and her Christian work in her prime. It will have served some of the writer's hopes if modern readers find here what Legh Richmond saw as an objective in reading the life stories of others.

> "To know that others have been perplexed with the same doubts, alarmed by the same fears, animated by the same hopes, comforted by the same promises, and directed by the same precepts, will demonstrate a holy identity in the influence of the Gospel and the effects produced by it; and may comfort the trembling sinner and confirm the most advanced believer."

(Quoted from *Domestic Portraiture,* p224, in one of the surviving notebooks of Emily Gosse.)

Chapter 1 – The Black Falls

Someone touring Mid-Wales nowadays, who leaves Dolgellau by the A470 road northwards, will only have gone a few miles before he feels he must explore the National Trust land around the little village of Ganllwyd. In particular, he will want to see for himself in the Dolymelynllyn Estate, the renowned Y Rhaeadr Ddu falls. The Trust's guide booklet explains that, for centuries, these falls have acted as a magnet to travellers.

> These cascading falls... on the River Gamlan, with their canopy of dripping trees, have inspired generations of travellers, including well-known artists and poets. Richard Wilson and Thomas Gainsborough found their way here, despite the difficulties of travelling through the mountainous heart of "Wild Wales".

One such traveller wrote enthusiastically:

> Returning by the side of the Mawddach, I saw Mr Madocks' house. now occupied by Mr Woodcock, at Dolmelynllyn, or the Holm of the Yellow Pool, embosomed in a fine rich and extensive wood. I kept up the hills a considerable height for the purpose of ascertaining from thence the figure and character of Cader Idris; but a lowering sky disappointing me, I returned and crossed the Mawddach again into the public road; following which a short distance, I came to Rhyad Ddu, or Black Cataract, in the grounds of Dolmelynllyn on the furious river Gamlan. This is another celebrated fall, that gave me as much pleasure in the contemplation of it as any I had yet witnessed; but an insufficient quantity of water at the time rendered it less sublime than if better supplied. The character of it is bold, and receives much consequence from the beautiful lichen and variegated green of other trees spread about, and with the jet black rocks that lie in rude order, above and below, makes up a whole perhaps not excelled by its neighbouring rivals.[1]

This was how artist Edward Pugh described this popular beauty spot which is near Ganllwyd, some six miles north of Dolgellau, and now part of a National Trust property. It had attracted the admiration of William Madocks[2] after his father died in 1790, and he bought an area of land at the junction of the Gamlan and Mawddach river valleys along with two farms and their woodland. Soon he had an attractive cottage built on a wooded knoll and a path made to give good access to the falls. In 1798, though, he took on a larger project on the Caernarvonshire coast north of Harlech. This involved extensive land reclamation and, consequently, he went to live there and rented the cottage and land at Dolymelynllyn to a succession of tenants.

Another traveller charmed by the beauties of this district at that period was the diarist Richard Fenton who wrote as follows of his visit to it in September, 1808, in the course of his extensive tours in Wales:

> Stop at Dolymelynllyn to see the beautiful and picturesque falls on the Canfa, a river that has its course rather precipitous all the way, being, in the greatest part of it, much inclined to a cataract, but the two principal falls are just above an Alpine bridge over which you will go to W O Madocks's charming cottage. I question whether in all Wales there are two finer falls seen at once and so happily disposed of and with such rich accompaniment of wood and rock. ... Ride up to see the cottage which is most delightfully situated on a little knoll with pleasing swells and inequalities in the little lawn. The cottage has a verandah quite rustic about it, it consists of 3 rooms below, with offices behind, and bed chambers above. ... It is now occupied by a Mr Bowes.[3]

The Mr Bowes, to whom Fenton referred, was William Bowes who had identified Dolymelynllyn as an ideal setting for a new life for his family and himself away from the bustle of the City. His father, who had been successful in business and was a member of Lloyd's Insurance, died in 1805. So William was now ready for a new start. Once the formalities of leasing were completed, he moved to the cottage in 1807[4] with his wife, Hannah, and their daughter, Emily, who had been born on 10th November of the previous year. By coming to this place in Wales they would have a healthy and stimulating environment for the upbringing of their family, to which two more children were added, sons born there –

Edmund in 1808, and Arthur in 1813.[5] While Hannah was occupied with the care of their children, and of their home there, William was devoting himself to the farms, gardens and sixty acres of woodland. In 1835 Emily recalled in her journal that she had once had a narrow escape while riding on a pony that trotted off from her father's care, and she had to hold on, as well as a three-year-old could, until her mother and nurse managed to stop it.

When Emily was married and living in London, she made use of another recollection of her childhood in Wales in a Gospel tract she wrote, which was also published in a French translation,

> When I was a child my father kept sheep; and I well remember the shepherd coming into the house with a little lamb, whose mother had died. The lamb was given to me, and being brought up by hand, grew very fond of me. It would follow me everywhere like a dog. One day, however, I was walking with my nurse through a wood, and my lamb strayed from me. I ran, and I called, but to no purpose, and then I was obliged to leave it. I often returned, and sometimes caught a glimpse of it, but it had grown quite wild, and chose to live in the woods. Whether it ended its days there, or whether it was ever caught and killed by the country people (which is most probable), so far as I was concerned, it was for ever lost; and lost, not because its young shepherd was indifferent to its fate, but because "It did not love the shepherd's voice, It did not love the fold."[6]

Another reminiscence has been preserved by Emily in one of her poems, "Lines in an old Bible", which was published in 1834.

> She, who first this book possessed
> Long has been a spirit blessed;
> Mid earth's sorrows, toil, and strife,
> By this book she ruled her life,
> Till in heaven she proved its truth;
> Then 'twas sent to guide my youth.

'Twas in childhood my delight,
'Neath my pillow laid at night;
From its page my task I said,
In it to my parents read.
Thence I learnt in early youth,
To revere the God of truth.

Saviour! may its sacred page
Bless me through life's pilgrimage!
May I by the rules there given,
Pass each hour from hence to heaven;
And till death, still hold the truth
Which enlightened first my youth![7]

This tranquil life in Wales lasted barely seven years though, for Mr Bowes' capital evaporated in 1814, apparently as a result of one of the many shipping losses suffered by Lloyd's members in that period.[8] For the next twenty years or more, the family lived modestly in the south of England with the generous help of several friends. Among those benefactors were the Elfords of Plymouth. Sir William Elford[9] had been the Lieutenant Colonel of the South Devon Militia in Ireland while William Bowes served as a Captain in the same regiment. Sir William's son, Jonathan,[10] who was Emily's godfather, provided her with an annuity of £25 for the next ten years. This gift contributed largely to her education, equipping her to serve later as a governess from 1824 to 1841.

William and Hannah had come through considerable hardship in what had been turbulent years for both of them in their respective childhoods, which must have fitted them to cope all the more effectively with a recurrence of such in married life. Something of their story must now be told.

Notes

1   Edward Pugh, A *Tour through North Wales,* London, 1816, p 181.

2   William Alexander Madocks, 1774-1828.

3   Richard Fenton, *Tours in Wales,* 1804-1813, p 117. A water colour drawing by Moses Griffith of the cottage at that period is held by the National Library of Wales, Aberystwyth.

4 Edmund Gosse, *Father and Son,* p 2, states that William Bowes bought a little estate on the slopes of Snowdon. Dolymelynllyn is, however, some twenty miles from Snowdon. It was leased, and not sold, to Bowes. Earlier, Gosse wrote that Bowes had inherited this property, *The Life of P H Gosse,* pp 215, 216. See also Elizabeth Beazley, *Madocks and the Wonder of Wales.*

5 Emily was born at 74 Great Portland Street and baptised at St Marylebone Parish Church on 31st January, 1807; Edmund Elford and Arthur were born at Dolymelynllyn and baptised at the ancient parish church in Llanelltyd which, incidentally, has an unusual circular graveyard.

6 *Thomas Winter's Stray Sheep,* p 2. Poem adapted from *I was a wandering sheep,* by H Bonar.

7 E[mily] B[owes], *Hymns and Sacred Poems,* Bath, 1834. It is very likely that the Bible had belonged to her maternal grandmother, Sarah Troutbeck, who died at Hingham, Massachusetts on 26th August in 1813 aged 77.

8 Ann Thwaite, in *Glimpses of the Wonderful* p 149, goes further than the notoriously unreliable Edmund Gosse in writing that this was through "gambling on the turf". He had written in *Father and Son* p 3 of his grandfather's "reckless expenditure, which he never checked till ruin was upon him." The evidence from Lloyd's and from his friends is quite to the contrary.

9 William Elford, 1749-1837, banker, MP.

10 Jonathan Elford, 1776-1823.

11 Edmund Gosse, in *Father and Son,* p 16, says that his mother "in spite of an extreme dislike of teaching, which was native to her, immediately accepted the situation of a governess in the family of an Irish nobleman." But on the contrary, she regarded teaching as a great delight, in fact, she took up the governess post ten years after the financial crash, and the Irish nobleman is an invention of Edmund's.

Chapter 2 – Loyalty and its Costs

As Captain Edward Le Cras brought HMS *Somerset*[1] into Torbay in South Devon on 8th February 1776, surely no one could have been more relieved to climb the Brixham harbour steps than the chaplain, the Revd. John Troutbeck and his family[2]. The 64-gun man-of-war had crossed the North Atlantic battered by wild gales, heavy seas and driving rain. Leaving Halifax, Nova Scotia, on 15th January, the ship had suffered extensive damage to her masts, sails and rigging, and a few of the crew had even been lost overboard.

Revd John Troutbeck was born at Great Blencow in Cumberland in 1718, the third son of farmer George Troutbeck and his wife Mary. After graduating at Queen's College, Oxford, he was ordained by the Bishop of Lincoln with title to the rural parish of Yelden[3] in Bedfordshire on 20th September, 1741. Thirteen years later, with the royal bounty of £20, he was licensed by the Bishop of London to serve as a missionary in Hopkinton, Massachusetts, but he resigned from his missionary post in 1755 to become the assistant of Dr Henry Caner at King's Chapel in Boston. On 8th May, 1759 he and Sarah Gould, the daughter of a Boston merchant, were married at that chapel and they might well have spent the rest of their days together there but for the dispute between Britain and her American colonies. Like Dr Caner, Troutbeck's sympathies lay on the Loyalist side, and he was one of 96 signatories of the Loyal Address to Governor Thomas Gage in 1775. With their daughters, Sarah who was born in 1760, and Hannah who was born in 1768, John and Sarah Troutbeck sailed out of Boston aboard the *Somerset* on 21st August, 1775 to take refuge in Halifax, Nova Scotia. There they were to spend the next five months awaiting their passage to England. Back in Boston their property was confiscated by the state and he was declared banished.[4] The total value of the property was estimated at between £20,000 and £23,000.

As a family the Troutbecks made their way from Devon to London where they could meet up with other Loyalists who had returned there and with whom they could discuss their plight.[5] When Thomas

Hutchinson saw him he described him to a friend as *much emaciated.*[6] In the evacuation of Boston on 17th March, some eleven hundred persons had left Boston and a total of six or seven thousand are believed to have reached Britain in the course of 1776,[7] many of whom appealed to Parliament for some aid to compensate for the loss of property and possessions on account of their loyalty to the Crown, but the processing of their appeals took several years.

In the case of the Revd John Troutbeck and his family, the Treasury did eventually decide on an annual payment of £150, and a curacy in Warwickshire brought him a further £50. A son was born in January 1777 and called John after his father, but the delighted parents had still more trials to face. On the way from London to Newcastle on one occasion, the collier on which the Revd Troutbeck was travelling, was captured by pirates. Then on 13th August, 1779 he died of tuberculosis at Great Blencow in Ennim Bank,[8] the house where he had been born sixty one years earlier. Having lived without financial constraints until four years before, it was humiliating for Sarah to continue having to beg for help from the Treasury who had now cut her allowance to £100. The health, too, of her young son gave further concern, and he died in December, 1781.

In her plight, Sarah considered that her best hope would be to obtain permission to return to America so she could try there to reclaim some of her former property. So, with her two daughters, Sarah now 24 and Hannah not yet 16, she sailed back to Boston in June 1784. There had been great changes in the nine years of her absence, and the new authorities were in no hurry to help her. By the summer of 1786 she was back in London with Hannah, still pursuing the British Treasury, while her elder daughter remained with friends in Boston. There are gaps in our knowledge of the years that followed. It appears that about 1790 Sarah saw that Hannah was settled reasonably in England and this allowed her to return to her daughter Sarah in Boston where she did recover some of her former property.

When the Revd John Troutbeck left Boston in August 1775, the rector, Dr Henry Caner,[9] remained there for another seven months endeavouring to provide pastoral care for those of his congregation who were still in the city. But the British forces found themselves in serious trouble and decided to evacuate. With no more than seven hours notice Dr Caner had to pack what he could and, with his daughter and a servant, leave for Halifax. They reached England later that year where he lived until 1792, when he died, aged 92.

Among other Loyalists who made for England, more is known about the travels and experiences of Samuel Curwen from his fascinating journal that survived to be published posthumously.[10] Leaving his wife Abigail in Salem, he sailed from Delaware Bay on 22nd May, 1775, and came ashore at Dover on 3rd July. During the voyage he carefully chronicled what he observed of the sky, the weather conditions and the behaviour of the ship and its crew. Over the next nine years he recorded his impressions of the people and places he met with in the course of his extended itinerary in England.

Another family that left New England at the Boston evacuation in March 1776 was that of William Bowes, a local merchant. He had taken the Loyalist side and was an addresser of both Governors Hutchinson and Gage. During the siege he was involved along with the British military, and left with them for Halifax. His wife had died on 9th May, 1774 leaving him with the care of their son William and daughter Sarah, both of them under four years of age. Mr Bowes was much in contact with other exiles in England and soon made his home in Hoddesdon in Hertfordshire from which he could reach London easily. Mr Hugh Hughes of the Grange, Hoddesdon,[11] had entertained quite a number of Loyalists while they tried to decide about their future. Hoddesdon was also an attractive place for young William and Sarah's settling into English life. In 1787 William Bowes moved with his family into London to live at 4 New Street, Bishopsgate. This was convenient for the promotion of his business, Bowes, Codner & Ravenhill at Coopers Row as wine merchants and insurance brokers. He became a member of Lloyd's Insurance in 1800.

Meanwhile, William junior clearly having some of his father's sense of loyalty, volunteered in 1797 for service with the recently formed South Devon Militia, to be made a lieutenant on 18th March, 1798. But he had interests in another direction too. On 10th April he was married, by licence, to Hannah Troutbeck at St Marylebone Parish Church.[12] William senior, however, did not approve of the marriage for some reason that has not been made clear. The two families were well known to each other and Mr Bowes had, on at least two occasions, acted as a witness for Mrs Troutbeck in her correspondence with the British Treasury. Possibly the young couple hoped that Mr Bowes would come to accept his son's marriage during the course of the emergency of the Militia service, but that was not to be. The regiment was part of the south coast defences and was on the point of being sent to Ireland in June 1798 to help put down the rebellion there and deal with a landing of French military, but this was postponed until 2nd September when they embarked for Waterford. Their ten months' service was highly praised by the citizens of Waterford who had a silver medal struck in their honour. On returning to England the Militia toured and paraded in the following years along the south coast, and up to the north as far as Liverpool.

In the meantime Hannah took the opportunity of joining her mother in America until her father-in-law's death in May 1805. After his father's estate, which was valued at £15,000, was settled, young William too was elected a member of Lloyd's Insurance, and he and Hannah made their home in London. A year later, Sarah Troutbeck and her elder daughter decided on an extended European tour going as far as Leipzig, and, of course, allowing time in London to greet and admire baby Emily, Sarah's first grandchild. The future for William and Hannah now held great promise. An attractive little estate was available for rent in Merioneth-shire, and so they set up house in lovely Dolymelynllyn. For seven years they could revel in their idyllic surroundings, but then with their financial crash everything was to change. William and Hannah had now to face a trauma that would have brought back memories of the hardships that had followed their hurried departure from Boston thirty-eight years before. Little Emily was only a few months older than her mother had been when she stepped ashore at Brixham. Hannah's training would now play an important part in the spiritual development of Emily that prepared her to express herself later in her poem:

> When anxious cares disturb my soul,
> And grief's dark clouds above me roll;
> When by foreboding fears oppressed,
> In vain I seek for peace or rest;
> How sweet to know I have a friend,
> Whose love and pity have no end.

> O Jesus! man's unchanging friend,
> To me thy favours still extend!
> In death and life, in weal and woe,
> Thy wonted kindness ever show;
> And in return thy name I'll praise,
> And dedicate to thee my days![13]

Notes

1 See M H Gibson: *H M S Somerset*, 1746-1778, Cotuit, Mass, 1992, for a description of that ship and its history.

2 On 5th November, 1688, it was in rather different circumstances that Prince William of Orange climbed the same steps at Brixham harbour to a warm welcome. "As the tide was low, the boat could not approach close enough for the party to land. Whereupon a little man waded into the water, and taking the Prince on his shoulders carried him to the steps of the quay." *Torquay Directory*, 31st October, 1888.

3 William Dell, an earlier incumbent, had been ejected from the charge in 1662. His parishioners complained that he had allowed John Bunyan to preach in the church on Christmas Day in 1659.

4 J H Stark: *The Loyalists of Massachusetts*, Boston, 1810, p 279.

5 A favourite meeting place was the New England Coffee House in Fleet Street.

6 P O Hutchinson: *Diary and Letters of Thomas Hutchinson*, p 199.

7 M B Norton: *The British Americans*, p 36.

8 Ennim Bank was the home of Lord and Lady Whitelaw.

9 L Sabine: *The American Loyalists*, Boston, 1847, p 199.

10 A Oliver: *The Journal of Samuel Curwen*, Cambridge, USA, 1972.

11 *Herts Countryside:* February, 1978, pp 16, 17.

12 Edmund Gosse in his *Life of P H Gosse*, p 215, is incorrect in much that he writes there about his grandfather, William Bowes, for example, when he says that he had been "hurried away [from Boston] by his parents, whose nerves the tea party had shaken, to North Wales where the family settled in the neighbourhood of Snowdon." But William Bowes' mother had died a year before the evacuation of Boston, and his father never went consequently to live in Wales. Gosse also states that his grandfather "had been forced to be a loyalist in vain for once grown to man's estate he went back for a wife and secured a New Englander as true as himself." The sequence of events as described in this chapter is quite different, and, of course, the bride's father, Revd John Troutbeck, was an Englishman.

13 Consolatory Thoughts, E[mily] B[owes]: *Hymns and Sacred Poems*, 1832, p 17.

Chapter 3 – Learning and Teaching

As recounted in chapter one, Jonathan Elford gave an annuity of £25 to Emily before she and her family left Wales. He also gave her a large family Bible[1] on the front of which she wrote, "Sanctify me through thy truth, thy word is truth." It now bears also an inscription in her brother's handwriting, "Emily Bowes, 7th April, 1814, from her Godfather, Jonathan Elford Esq ..." When she left Merionethshire for Devon she was setting out on an uncharted path which would involve many more moves for her in the next ten years. She was a bright, intelligent child who might have expected her formal education to commence at the Girls' School in Dolgellau, but very different plans for it had now to be made. On 1st October, 1814, nine days before her eighth birthday, she left Dolgellau bound for Otterton where she would be in the care of the Shore family. The Revd Thomas William Shore[2] had been vicar of the parish since his installation in it on 11th July, 1793 and his daughter took in hand the teaching of the new arrival over the next six or seven months.

The River Otter rises in the Blackdown Hills on the borders of Devon and Somerset, and traces its twenty mile course to reach the sea at Budleigh Salterton. Centuries ago, before the river's mouth was silted up, Otterton had been an active fishing port. The Otterton Mill, which was rebuilt in the 1970s, had been in operation from the eleventh century until 1958. It stands today with its ancient water wheels each nine metres in diameter, a reminder to modern visitors of the sounds and industry at the heart of that village in the nineteenth century. In 1814 when there were just over two hundred families in the parish the children's education was provided locally by one Parochial Boys' School and by separate Boys' and Girls' Sunday Schools. In Emily's recollection of her stay with the Shores, in later years she wrote, "Miss Shore taught me the elements of learning, and my mind was greatly opened."

On 3rd May, 1815 she was able to rejoin her mother and brothers who had come to reside at Exmouth in the estate of Lord John Rolle who had been the Commanding Officer of the South Devon Militia during the term of William Bowes' service in it. We can expect that, on a clear day when Hannah Bowes could look along the coast towards Berry Head, she would describe to her children how she had first set foot on English soil forty years before when she was brought ashore from the *Somerset* at Brixham. Hannah also took Emily several times to Lady Glenorchy's Chapel[3] at Exmouth where she was deeply impressed both by the Presbyterian services and by the preaching there of the Revd Robert Winton. In later years Emily was strongly influenced by the published letters and memoirs of the Revd Legh Richmond, but it was at Exmouth that she was first introduced to his writings when she was given a copy of his popular Gospel booklet, *The Young Cottager*. The moving story of the simple faith of twelve year old Jenny of Brading in the Isle of Wight gripped Emily and she read it over and over again. She was so impressed by Willam Law's *Serious Call to a Devout and Holy Life* that she took up its practical suggestions for a disciplined practice of Bible reading and private prayer. By applying herself to this she could soon repeat most of the Psalms by heart. Recognising her earnestness, Miss Russell, one of her teachers, gave her many books and encouraged her further by committing to her the main responsibility of the Sunday School when she was only nine years old.

Although in adult life Emily described her education as "irregular", yet by the help of more than half a dozen interested Devon friends she was taught a good range of subjects for her age. Major Algernon Langton,[4] for example, gave her lessons in German and Miss Cooke made no charge for receiving her into her school where she taught her French. In her last year at Exmouth a group of those generous friends put her to school there. Later she could recall with gratitude that it was "mercifully ordered that neither my maintenance, clothes or education has ever been an expense to my parents since their circumstances were reduced."

For the latter years of Emily's education the family moved to London on 19th April, 1819, taking lodgings firstly in Marylebone Street. Here they attended the church[5] which had been completely rebuilt since they left London in 1807. Emily and her brother Edmund attended their respective schools and for most of their first year their aunt, Sarah Bowes, was living within reach in Great Portland Street. Extended visits were made to Warwick at Christmas between 1819 and 1823. Then, early in 1824 preparations were made for Emily's first employment as a governess. With her mother she left London by coach in mid February for

Newbury and on to Highclere where they stayed until 2nd March when Emily took up her post at the rural rectory of Compton Beauchamp nearby. And now a most important period in her life was about to take shape.

Notes

1 This was an 1807 edition of the Authorised Version, published by Oxford University Press, with Apocrypha and marginal references, handsomely bound in red leather with gilt embossing. There are numerous handwritten annotations in it relating to chronology and interpretation inserted by Emily in the course of her years of study of it.

2 Revd Thomas William Shore (1756-1823), brother of Lord Teignmouth (1751–1834), Governor General of India and first president of the British and Foreign Bible Society.

3 Samuel Curwen, whom we met in chapter two, had visited the chapel on 18th July, 1779 and recorded in his journal, "Attended worship at Lady Glenorchy's Chapel; principles inculcated not unlike those at Lady Huntingdon's chapels. The preacher, a Scotchman, a missionary of Lady G., who, with Mr Holmes of Exeter, fitted the chapel for the propagation of Scotch orthodoxy." *Journal and Letters,* 1845, page 221. The chapel had only been founded ten years before, in 1777.

4 Son of Bennet Langton (1737-1801), and Mary, Dowager Countess of Rothes (1743-1820).

5 It was in St Marylebone Parish Church that Emily's parents had been married on 10th April, 1798, there too she was baptised on 31st January, 1807, and it was there that the funeral service of her son, Edmund, was held in May 1928.

▌Chapter 4 – Teaching and Learning

I t was to the ancient little village of Highclere that seventeen-year-old Emily and her mother came in February, 1824. Its history had begun with a Saxon Charter of 749 in which King Cuthred of Wessex granted lands to the church founded earlier that year. Emily's history was entering a new stage too, as she set out on her working life hardly knowing that she was to spend fourteen years of it in the Vale of the White Horse.

One of those who was to influence her during that time was the energetic young curate of Highclere, the Revd Alexander Robert Charles Dallas.[1] He had come to the parish in September, 1821 and was quite immersed in his work there. In later years he would be especially involved in the founding of the Society for Irish Church Missions for which he was instrumental in the erection of 21 churches and 49 school-houses, a work which Emily keenly supported. Of this critical period she later appreciatively recorded the help Mr Dallas's counsel had been to her.

Her days at Highclere allowed her a trip to Wantage, daily visits to Mrs Dallas, and one to Newbury to meet her new employer, the Revd John C C P Hawkins,[2] the curate of Compton Beauchamp. That meeting was successful and the date of her engagement was fixed for Tuesday, 2nd March, 1824.

The parish of Compton Beauchamp had just over a hundred residents on its 1811 acres when Emily went there. It was formed in a long strip stretching from the northern edge of the Lambourn Downs to the low lying fields in the Vale of the White Horse. The adjoining parish was that of Uffington where the vicar was Dr Thomas Hughes, grandfather of Thomas Hughes the writer of *Tom Brown's Schooldays*. Of greater interest to us is that author's work on The Scouring of the White Horse which was published in 1859. It describes the local practice of scouring, or refurbishing, the 374 feet long horse which was cut in the hillside of chalk. This refurbishing was done only once while Emily was there, in 1825.

The main part of the little church of St Swithun with its bell tower goes back to the 13th century and has been added to over the years, but yet it is still possible to picture now the scene in the 1820s. Two services were held in it each Sunday. The morning service was at 11am, and the afternoon one alternated between 2pm and 3.30pm to allow Mr Hawkins to conduct fortnightly services in Longcott at 1.30pm, and at Shrivenham at 3pm. The celebration of the Lord's Supper was held four times a year, and the Rector, the Revd Robert Wintle of Culham, visited annually.

When Emily came to Compton Beauchamp, there were four girls and one boy in the Hawkins family and, while she was there, four more boys and three more girls were added so that she had plenty to occupy her as governess to all these children.

And Emily's active mind was also well occupied in her leisure hours. She took lessons in music, drawing and Hebrew,[3] and was also an avid reader. She read and copied into her notebook from the poetry of Charlotte Elizabeth, John Keble, John Moultrie, Henry Francis Lyte and others with titles such as, *To hope, Ode to forgetfulness, Submission, Pleading with God,* and *Speak gently.* Her interest in missions was shown by her extended quotations from the biographies of John Frederic Oberlin and Felix Neff,[4] both of which had been recently published in England. There are quotations of various lengths, too, from John Howe, John Owen, Philip Henry and John Flavel. One subject to which she gave close attention was that of unfulfilled prophecy. At that time she was following the writings of T R Birks and E B Elliott, making extensive quotations from the former and from Allison's *History of Europe during the French Revolution.* She also copied from M M Butt's *Lady of the Manor* half a dozen prayers dealing with subjects such as, Sincerity, Serious thoughts on Religion, and Thy will be done. These still carry a freshness to the reader today nearly two centuries later.

Emily's Confirmation took place in 1825 and, while there are no details of the event, it is known that Dr Thomas Burgess, the Bishop of Salisbury, conducted Confirmations "with a carefulness quite remarkable at that time."[5] She was able to have time off which allowed her to visit Bath on several occasions, and London, once her parents had set up house there about 1831. On these visits she made a practice of attending the preaching of prominent evangelical preachers of the time. She noted that at Bath she had listened to Mr Fenwick, Mr Wilson, Mr H Marriott and Mr W Jay, and that in London she had heard Mr D Wilson, Mr Sumner, Mr Fell, Mr Main and Mr Edward Irving.

Thomas Hughes, in *Tom Brown's Schooldays,* which was first published in 1857, the year of Emily's death, heads its first page with the couplet,

> I'm the Poet of White Horse Vale, sir,
> With liberal notions under my cap.

Hughes, born in 1822, would have been a contemporary of the Hawkins' children who were in Emily's care and he may well have known her in that capacity. It is doubtful, however, if he may even have known that she wrote poetry and that 126 of her poems had been published in two little volumes in 1832 and 1834. She had started writing them in 1829 and had resolved in 1831 to have them published. She shows in them considerable versatility in style and in content as well as a clear insight into the spiritual lessons to be drawn from them.

Perhaps it was to be expected that she should also turn her attention to the 1662 Book of Common Prayer, and render five of its Collects into verse. She does this with a liberty that is not closely tied to the wording of the original and yet succeeds in bringing out their meaning satisfactorily. In several of her poems proper she acknowledges also her need of divine help in her daily tasks; in *Of such is the kingdom of God*, for example, she expresses this in a fine prayer.

> Thou biddest me to teach and pray,
> Thou bidd'st me watch them night and day,
> And guard their minds from every ill;
> Then wilt thou not *thy* part fulfil,
> And every hurtful weed remove
> That checks the growth of heavenly love?
> And wilt thou not thine aid extend,
> To me their guardian and their friend?
> O teach me all I ought to say!
> Improve my judgment day by day!
> Increase my love; my labours bless,
> And crown them with complete success![6]

That the subject of overseas missions[7] exercised her mind considerably is shown by her devoting eight of her poems to the subject with titles such as, *The duty of prayer for missionaries,* and *A missionary hymn,* and *A missionary prayer.* Emily also made use of her own surroundings to find lessons for herself. *The Bees,* and *The lily of the valley,* are examples of this.

So, too, Emily records her thankfulness in an eight-verse poem entitled *Thanksgiving* which begins,

> Thanks to thee for every blessing
>   Which thy bounteous hand bestows;
> O the joy, Lord, of confessing
>   Whence my smallest comfort flows.

She rounds it off with

> Much I love, O Lord, confessing
>   Whence my every comfort flows.
> Still then shower on me such blessing
>   Which thy kindness now bestows.[8]

There are poems of self-scrutiny, like, *For a passionate person,* and *Confession,* and there are humble expressions of repentance, such as,

> But Oh, I humbly would intreat
>   That all my present pain
> May teach me that though sin be sweet,
>   Its end is worse than vain.
> Ne'er may it, now I've felt its sting
> My soul again to bondage bring.[9]

But she takes special delight in rendering the Psalms into verse. Her version of Psalm 22 shows a fine mastery of the psalmist's argument. In a lengthy treatment of *Abraham's temptation* in Genesis 22, Emily blends a gentle imagination with a deep insight into the significance of that intense testing of the Patriarch's faith.

There are amongst these poems of hers many prayers for personal peace, for forgiveness, and for patience, but it is her *Prayer for a happy death*[10] which perhaps most touches the reader who will soon be reading what the answer to that prayer would entail some twenty-three years in the future.

Notes

1   A R C Dallas, 1791-1869; see Anne B Dallas, *Incidents in the life and ministry of the Revd Alex R C Dallas,* 2nd ed. Nisbet, London, 1872.

2   John Cunningham Calland Popkin Hawkins, 1793-1871; see *The Marlborough Times, 2nd December;* 1871.

3   Her knowledge of Hebrew is shown in *Abraham and his children,* p 157.

4   For J F Oberlin, 1740-1826, see T Sims, *Memoirs of J F Oberlin,* London, 1830. For Felix Neff, 1798-1829, see W S Gilly, *Memoirs of Felix Neff; pastor of the high Alps,* London, 1832.

5   *Dictionary of National Biography,* vol vii p 313, article Thomas Burgess, 1756-1837.

6   E[mily] B[owes]: *Hymns and Sacred Poems,* Bath, 1832.

7   Edmund Gosse in *Father and Son,* p 25, surprisingly says that his mother was "cold about foreign missions" when the evidence is strongly the other way.

8   E[mily] B[owes]: *Hymns and Sacred Poems,* Bath, 1834.

9   Repentance, E[mily] B[owes]: *Hymns and Sacred Poems,* Bath, 1832.

10 E[mily] B[owes]: *Hymns and Sacred Poems,* Bath, 1832.

Chapter 5 - Getting to London

The situation at Compton Beauchamp was clearly most enjoyable for Emily. Although she must have been fully occupied in her duties as governess, she was able in most years to make extended visits to Lymington, Southwell, Bath, Osbourne, Exeter, and, of course, London. Her parents and brothers were evidently much in her thoughts and prayers. Indeed, she mentioned them several times in her poems, as, for example,

> Chiefly, bless my parents, dear,
> Sanctify their hearts, and cheer;
> Guide them in life's smoothest ways,
> Guard and bless them all their days.
>
> Keep my brothers, in their youth
> Firmly in the paths of truth;
> May they youthful follies flee,
> May their hearts be fixed on Thee.[1]

Mr and Mrs Bowes gradually recovered from their financial troubles and, around 1831, they set up home at number 1 Valentine Cottages, Brook Street, in Upper Clapton.[2] This would today be approximately on the site of the modern primary school in Northwold Road. Their elder son, Edmund, was able to go to Cambridge as a sizar in 1835 and to graduate BA in 1841.[3] He had studied under Mr Lockwood at Mill Hill from 1819 to 1821 , a family friendship which lasted for several years. After his graduation he went to Rutland where he taught in a private school there for a number of years. Arthur, who was four years younger than Edmund, did not go to university but was occupied as a tutor while they lived in Clapton.

It must have been a wrench for Emily to leave the idyllic rural environment of Compton Beauchamp. She had gone there at the age of seventeen and grown into a mature Christian during her time there. The country setting allowed her to take early morning walks which gave her great pleasure, as she wrote in one of her poems,

> And great is my delight
> On Sabbath mornings bright
> To drink sweet draughts of dawn's reviving air;
> Unenviously I hear
> The sounds of slumberers near,
> I leave them all, and seek the garden fair.[4]

As mentioned earlier, when she went there in 1824 Mr and Mrs Hawkins had five children, four girls and a boy, the eldest being only seven. While she was there four more boys and three girls had been added, and a thirteenth was born after she left.[5] She would, therefore, have had a busy time in teaching all of them. Emily had not yet worked herself out of a job; it would appear to have been the urgent appeal in a particularly tragic situation elsewhere that led to her moving.

The Revd Christopher John Musgrave was the son of Sir John Chardin Musgrave of Eden Hall near Penrith. His brother, Sir Philip Musgrave, had inherited the baronetcy on the death of their father, and Christopher had gone into the ministry. He had become rector of Crundale parish in Kent in October 1825, and had married Marianne Hasell, a near Cumberland neighbour, in September 1826. Earlier that year he had successfully petitioned the Archbishop of Canterbury for permission to build a new rectory,[6] and he seems to have settled there into his life's work. Sadly, his brother died the following year and Christopher inherited the title. Consequently, he resigned his rectory and took up residence at the family home, Eden Hall. His energies were soon turned to the estate where he built a new lodge, and he repaired and extensively renovated Eden Hall church. But tragedy struck again. He died in May 1834, to be followed by his wife who died in September 1835.[7] Near neighbours of the Hasells of Dalemain were the Troutbecks of Great Blencow, cousins of Emily's grandfather. This was probably how the need for a governess was brought to Emily's attention when the children were taken to live with their aunt in Hove, in West Sussex.

It was in the spring of 1838 that Emily said her farewells to the Hawkins family to take up her new post as governess to the five Musgrave children under the care of their aunt, Miss Jane Hasell, at Brunswick Square in Hove. Georgiana, the eldest of the girls, was eleven then, and Fanny was only four. Life in Hove must have been very different from that in the parish of Compton Beauchamp. There were twelve Church of England and seven Independent churches in Brighton and Hove, and ten others, and a range of schools.[8] Few details have survived of her time at Hove, but after three years there, in the spring of 1841, Emily left for the parental home in Upper Clapton in London. Her mother by this time was quite infirm and very lame.

The number of Emily's references in her poetry and in her diaries to the uncertainty of life has been remarked upon,[9] but life expectancy was then only 40 years. There were proportionately very many who died under five years of age, but even between five and thirty-nine in 1820 248 out of a thousand died in England.[10] In her own circle her godfather, Jonathan Elford, had died in 1823 at the age of 47. The eldest of the Hawkins' sons died in Vienna of typhus fever when he was only thirty years old,[11] and, as we have already seen, the Revd Sir Christopher Musgrave died in 1834 aged 36, and Lady Musgrave a year later at the age of 34. Of the five Musgrave orphans, Edith, the third daughter died of "effusion on the brain" at the age of eighteen, and Fanny, the youngest, died of gastric fever when she was nineteen. Even Augusta, the second eldest, had a tragic early life. She married Colonel Henry Bonham in August 1850 but, to her great grief, he died in February 1856.[12] It was to her consolation that she later married the Earl of Stradbroke and settled at Henham Hall in Suffolk until his death in 1886.[13]

These were indeed times of change. William IV had died in June 1837 to be succeeded by his niece, the young Victoria, who married Prince Albert in 1840. The evangelical movement in the churches was growing. In the Society of Friends the tension between the "inner light" party and those who stressed the priority of evangelism resulted in numbers of secessions. In Tottenham, starch manufacturers Robert and John Elliot Howard left the Quakers to form an assembly of Brethren.[14] Their first meeting was held in a small room in Warner Terrace. In 1839 they built a chapel in Brook Street which was opened on the first Saturday of June that year and by 1842 there were 88 in communion. Meanwhile William Henry Dorman, the pastor of Islington Chapel had become concerned about the distinctions maintained between clergy and laity and between rich and poor in the congregation, and he resigned on 26th June to throw in his lot with the Brethren too. In Hackney a group of five men and five women met together on 4th July 1841 with the declaration, "Ten Christians commenced meeting for worship simply as such, and in the name of Jesus."[15] Very soon thereafter they were joined by Emily Bowes who would make this fellowship her spiritual home while in London which was to be for the rest of her life. On 16th September, writing to an American cousin, she described the Christians with whom she met as "not belonging to... any sect, but a collection of Christians who met as such out of all different sects, ...endeavouring to revive the brotherly love of the early Christians by persuading all who love the Lord Jesus Christ to meet together without quarrelling about their little differences, taking the Bible only as their rule of life, the Holy Spirit as their teacher, and God as their only head and master."

Notes

1 Intercession, E[mily] B[owes]: *Hymns and Sacred Poems*, Bath, !834.

2 In *Glimpses of the Wonderful,* p 357, Mrs Thwaite refers to the 1841 census entry in respect of the Bowes' residence which she reasons was in Tottenham, p352. The census, however, describes it as Upper Clapton in the Parish of Hackney, in the Borough of Tower Hamlets, reference HO 107/700.

3 Alum Cantab Volume II p 342. He published *A Key to Henry's First Latin Book (by T K Arnold)* ; F & J Rivington, London, 1851. Edmund Gosse in *Father and Son,* p 16, says that his mother was "several years senior" to her brother, Edmund, whereas there were only 23 months between them.

4 Sunday Morning, E[mily] B[owes]: *Hymns and Sacred Poems,* Bath, 1834.

5 Census 1841, reference HO 107/27. Curiously Ann Thwaite in *Glimpses of the Wonderful,* p 161, says that Emily had "seen the arrival and progress of eleven babies in her fourteen years as a governess..."

6 Vicar General Act Book, Volume XIV, pp 554,555,577, 583; Volume XV, p 71.

7 Burke's *Peerage and Baronetcy,* 1986, p2546. *The Cumberland Pacquet* May 6th and 13th, 1834, and September 8th 1835. Ann Thwaite in *Glimpses of the wonderful,* p 151, mistakenly calls him Sir Charles Musgrave of Brighton.

8 Leppard's *Brighton Directory,* 1839, p 117.

9 D Wertheimer PhD thesis, *Philip Gosse,* 1810-1888 ...p 166.

10 *Annual Register,* 1820.

11 *Marlborough Times,* 2nd December, 1871.

12 *Sussex Advertiser,* 3rd September, 1850; R S Liddell, *The Memoir of the Tenth Royal Hussars,* London 1891.

13 *The Times,* 29th January, 1886, p 7.
14 Henry Pickering, *Chief Men among the Brethren,* London nd *p 58.*
15 I am indebted to Dr David Brady of Rylands Library, University of Manchester, for this information.

Chapter 6 - Ripening into Love

There was an enthusiasm about the little group who first met at Ellis's Room in Hackney on 4th July, 1841. This was a new beginning, and on most Sundays they were joined by other evangelical Christians from the area. Within two years about fifty were meeting together on Sundays, and by about 1847 such was the attendance that it was necessary to move into the School room in St Thomas's Square. In early 1856 they purchased for themselves Providence Chapel in Paragon Road which would serve them for many years to come.

Among the original members was George Pearse,[1] a jobbing stockbroker. He threw himself into a range of evangelistic causes while he was at Hackney. In particular, he acted as honorary secretary of the Chinese Evangelisation Society under whose auspices James Hudson Taylor first sailed for China. In 1868, when Pearse was 57, he gave up business and went to Paris with his wife to witness among French soldiers and to set up a depot for the distribution of Scriptures, Gospel tracts, etc., at 4 Place de Theatre Francais. In 1876 he visited Algeria but, finding no openings among the soldiers there, he turned his attention to the Kabyle people. In consultation with his friend Dr Grattan Guinness, he commenced a work there which remained close to his heart until his death in 1902.

Another active participant at the chapel from the beginning was William Thomas Berger[2] of Upper Homerton, the son of Samuel Berger, a colour and starch manufacturer. He had been converted in 1833 at the age of nineteen, and had soon become deeply involved in the promotion and support of evangelistic efforts both in Britain and overseas. He took a life-long interest in the China Inland Mission. On 4th April, 1843 he married Mary Van Sommer and, after an extended honeymoon tour, they set up house at Well Street, Hackney. For some years to come informal Bible Readings were held in evenings in their home where most of those attending were conversant with Classical Greek and some with Hebrew.

It was into this happy atmosphere that Emily Bowes came in 1841, and where she found mutual stimulation to engage in evangelistic work in the Capital. As she was, as we have discovered, of such a friendly, sympathetic disposition, she quickly won the confidence of those with whom she spoke in her journeys by omnibus or train, and in the course of her ordinary encounters. As Anna Shipton recalled, "The love of God in Christ beamed through her words and life, like sunshine melting away the clouds of prejudice. ...It was pre-eminently Jesus that she preached, his beauty, his loving kindness, his tender mercy."[3]

She had been particularly a diligent student of prophecy since she had been at Compton Beauchamp and had accepted the historicist interpretation of Revelation as expounded by T R Birks and E B Elliott. In 1843, however, Benjamin Wills Newton of Ebrington Street Chapel in Plymouth had brought out the first edition of his *Thoughts on the Apocalypse* in which he expounded a futurist interpretation, and, thanks to a visit to Plymouth, about that year, or the next, Emily had become taken with what her husband later described as the "beautiful and elaborate system of that eminent teacher," According to Mr Elliott's scheme of interpretation the major part of Revelation had already been fulfilled by events, whereas that of Mr Newton maintained that from Revelation 6 everything was still to be fulfilled in the future. Emily, however, gave up Mr Newton's interpretation largely through her reading of John Nelson Darby's *Examination* of it although he favoured a futurist viewpoint too. She later returned to Birks' and Elliott's historicist interpretation.[4]

Anna Shipton, who knew Emily only in her later years, described her as follows, "She was fair, and appeared more youthful for her years; from her small delicate features and the artless child-like smile which lighted her countenance when animated. I have seen it literally sparkling with joy when unexpectedly brought into contact with those who loved her Lord, or recognizing some expression of His ever watchful care... I felt for the first time the power of the life of a child of God walking with Him in cheerful child-like confidence in His love."[5]

Now into the Hackney circle on 9th July, 1843 had come one who would be in the future her devoted husband. He was Philip Gosse,[6] a young naturalist, and teacher in a small private school. After spending fourteen years in North America, he had returned to England where he had published in 1840 the first of some 36 fuller works, *The Canadian Naturalist*. In 1844 he went to Jamaica to study especially its bird life and published *Birds of Jamaica* in 1847. In 1950 it was still described as "not only a reliable, but also an indispensable guide to the modern student, even now a hundred years after it was written."[7]

Philip Gosse had been brought up in Poole where he had come under the ministry of the Revd Thomas Durant at Skinner Street Chapel. It was in the early years of that ministry that a young apprentice draper, John Angell James, had his first religious impressions which led to his becoming the popular minister of Carr's Lane Chapel, Birmingham from 1805 to his death in 1859,[8] Philip Gosse and Emily had become more and more acquainted since 1843 and he could write to his brother William telling him of his feelings on 21st October, 1848, and saying, "mutual respect has ripened into love." And so it followed that on 23rd November, 1848 they were married at Brook Street Chapel, Tottenham, by Mr Robert Howard, who entertained them afterwards to a wedding breakfast. Emily's two brothers were witnesses at the ceremony.

Notes

1   George Pearse was born on 5th June, 1815, and died on 30th June, 1902. For more details see *North Africa* , August, 1902, pp 85, 86.

2   For W T Berger see T C F Stunt, "James Van Sommer" in *Christian Brethren Research Journal*, August, 1967, pp 2-7.

3   Anna Shipton, *Tell Jesus, Recollections of Emily Gosse,* London, 1863, pp 18, 19.

4   P H Gosse *A Memorial of the last days on earth of Emily Gosse,* London, 1857, pp 16, 17.

5   Anna Shipton, *Tell Jesus,* London, 1863, pp 16, 17.

6   L R Croft, *Gosse: The Life of P H Gosse,* Preston, 2000.

7   R B Freeman and D Wertheimer, *P H Gosse: a bibliography*, Folkestone, 1979, p26.

8   R W Dale, *The Life of J A James* 1785-1859, London, 1861.

Chapter 7 – Writer and Poet

Marrying an established writer who was also a famous naturalist was greatly to alter the daily pattern of life for Emily, and yet it seemed to come naturally to her "to merge all her tastes and interests in" those of her husband, "so that she truly became a meet helper to him, and they walked together 'as heirs together of the grace of life.' "[1] Perhaps it was to be expected that she would then take up her own writing again which would fully occupy her in the remaining years of her life.

This is perhaps an appropriate point from which to look back again on the years she spent writing poems at Compton Beauchamp, for there was a similarity in the conditions of her writing in the 1850's to that in the 1830's. At both these periods she was particularly happy and contented with her environment, but in both situations she was inevitably somewhat constrained because of her commitments, though as the young governess she could use her leisure time in composing poetry, and as a young wife she could write Gospel tracts for the expanding distribution of such throughout the country and beyond.

In her poetry Emily varied her style considerably, and, while there may be technical flaws here and there, the spiritual content is exceedingly rich. A large proportion of the poems express her own inner thoughts and struggles as though initially they had been intended to be kept private, and some tell of her awareness of failures. There are frequent petitions, too, for a renewal of grace. In some a particular weakness is confessed, and help sought to overcome it in the future. One such is *Ill Spent Time.*

> Forgive me, O my God, I pray,
> The hours I've misemployed today;
> They ill thy scrutiny can stand,
> Ill bear the test of thy command;

She cannot bring back what is lost, even with tears, but

> Though you can ne'er lost time regain,
> Repentance is not useless pain;
> First let it lead to Jesus' feet,
> His pardon for the past to intreat;
> Then store its lessons in your mind
> To arm you, when to ill inclined.
> They oft must feel remorse's pain
> Who from the past no wisdom gain;
> But they who mourn o'er every crime
> Will conquer their defects in time.

The process is like that of the refiner working on some precious metal.

> For when the soul Christ's likeness shows,
> Its fitness for himself he knows.
> O to resemble him be mine,
> To wake, and in his image shine![2]

This humble self-scrutiny is to be found frequently in her poems, such as, *Confession, Deliver us from evil, Prayer for forgiveness, Repentance,* and others.[3]

Emily's care of the children features in her poems too. *Feed my sheep, Of such is the kingdom of God, On a child's death, On a little girl's birthday, Suffer the little children to come unto me,* all reveal how seriously she accepted her vocation, and how anxious she was to serve the Lord in it. Her poem, *The Snowdrop,* is a fine blend of the playful and the serious.

> Ah, little do you know, dear child,
> > How ill your words apply,
> When you compare this lovely flower
> > To such a one as I!
>
> The flower, (while I deep sunk in guilt,
> > Was sinful from my birth)
> Rose from her dark and miry tomb
> > Untinged by stain of earth.

She develops the contrast and concludes,

> Oh how unlike, then, are we not?
>   It seems like mockery
> To hear the snowdrop pure compared,
>   Though e'en in jest, to me.
>
> And yet, my love, although your type
>   Suits now, nor you, nor me,
> I feign will hope the hour may come
>   When we as pure may be.

The snowdrop's early life was spent hidden in the earth until,

> But suns unseen, its life renewed,
>   On rains scarce felt, it fed,
> Till, fitted for a purer life,
>   It spurned its lowly bed.

Might we look forward to such a transformation too?

> How soon, in robes as stainless white,
>   Our souls may be arrayed,
> And our glad brows, enwreathed with flowers,
>   Heaven's flowers, that never fade!
>
> Till then, to nought so pure, may we
>   Our sinful hearts compare;
> But, knowing not what we shall be
>   Lament for what we are![4]

There are special petitions as well, such as, *Consolation in distress, For a passionate person, No man can serve two masters,* and *Prayer for patience. Give us day by day, our daily bread,* strikes a telling plea for a contented spirit.

> O it is good, 'tis sweet to me,
> Thy pensioner, dear Lord, to be;
> And every day and hour to live
> On what thy charity may give.

Of worldly things, I ask no store,
Food when 'tis needed, not before,
A shelter from bleak winter's cold,
And rest from toil when I am old.

At night a pillow for my head,
In sickness, thee to make my bed,
A refuge in affliction's blast,
And hopes of bliss when life is past.

She does not ask for a year's supply today, but grace for a day at a time.

'Tis well, Lord, that it thus should be;
It draws the soul more near to thee.
And thus we two-fold blessings share,
Blessed in thy answer, blessed our prayer.[5]

Emily's poems cover a fair range of subjects. There are a good many expressing her praise and thanksgiving for God's blessings and providences in her own life, and there are eight which treat different aspects of overseas missions – a life-long interest of hers, as has been mentioned earlier.[6] In addition to her rendering into verse of the five Collects, the rendering mentioned in chapter four, she did the same with eighteen Psalms and with quite a number of other portions of Scripture too. In particular, her rendering in 268 lines of *Abraham's Temptation,* known to Jews as the Akedah, shows a rich blend of her skills of imagination and interpretation which must have been rare for a girl in her mid-twenties.

In the 1850's, when Emily resumed her writing, she devoted herself to two distinct outlets; firstly, to the insatiable demand for Gospel tracts, and, secondly, to supplying help and encouragement to busy young mothers. The latter outlet was chiefly through a magazine called *The Mother's Friend: a monthly magazine to aid and encourage those mothers who have little time to read, and little money to spend.* For this she started writing in 1853 and contributed, in all, nearly a dozen articles, the last four being published posthumously.

There are short pieces cautioning against leaving children in the care of girls who are unreliable, or commending a young mother who is determined to persevere in her sewing at home because of her husband's delicate health. She tells the story, in simple graphic language, of a blind Irishman who was converted through having bought a Bible for his grandson to read to him. Again, she relates the account of the conversion of a girl who had been led to faith in Jesus Christ through her providential encounter with a verse from a hymn by Isaac Watts, and later a Gospel tract. She had to find employment in a Christian home when her parents turned her out, but was glowing with the joy of her salvation when she told her story to Emily.

For most of 1852 the family was away from London in Devon, where Philip Gosse occupied himself in collecting and examining specimens of marine life. They stayed from 27th January of that year at St Marychurch until late April when they moved to Ilfracombe for the next six months. One fine day they engaged a horse-drawn carriage to take them the fifteen miles from Ilfracombe to Lynton and back. The purpose of the trip was to explore the Valley of the Rocks and view the landscape from Castle Rock. Emily described their journey in a delightful article, the fourth of a series, in SPCK's magazine, *Home Friend,* and in 1853 the series appeared together as *Seaside Pleasures,* the other three chapters having been written by her husband.

Not long after this, Emily was contemplating her one larger book. It was a 235 page work published by Nisbet & Co with the title *Abraham and his Children: or Parental duties illustrated by Scriptural examples.* In the Introduction she acknowledges that our children are being educated by us, however unwittingly, through the example of our whole behaviour. It is vital, therefore, that such example should be directed by the principles found in Scripture. "In the following pages the writer has endeavoured to glean a few of the treasures of divine wisdom on this subject, even the wisdom of Him who is the Father of Lights who giveth to all men liberally (James 1: 5, 17). May more of his countenance shine on the writer and the reader ."[7]

In its twenty-three chapters Emily examined the lives of several characters, from Abraham to Lois and Eunice, drawing out of them exhortations and warnings for today's parents. There are many gems in the pages of this work. For example, "There is no way of obviating the disadvantages of riches except by using them for God" p 47; or "That faith only is unfeigned faith which manifests its reality by acting on the Word of God as unquestionably true," p 225. It is noteworthy that on four occasions she quotes from the writings of the Revd Charles Bridges (1794-1869), a life-long friend of the Revd A R C Dallas (1791-1869) with whom Emily had kept in touch since her days at Highclere in 1824. It was Charles Bridges who had preceded him in his curacy of Wooburn. There is another influence traceable in the whole tenor of this book, that of the Revd Legh Richmond (1772-1827). It was the reading of his *The Young Cottager* which had greatly impressed her as a child at Exmouth, as already mentioned above, and, at Compton Beauchamp, she had copied out large portions from his *Domestic Portraiture.* Emily earnestly sought to practise the lessons she was teaching; how tragic it is that she was to be removed so early in her parenthood!

It was, however, to writing Gospel tracts that Emily was especially attracted, and she entered into writing them with great enthusiasm. We know of 63 tracts that came from her pen from 1854 to 1856. Nearly half of these were accounts of encounters with people whom she met in travel when she would lead the conversation on to discuss spiritual matters, and some are of those who told her of their conversion. In them she dealt in a direct way with the issues of sin, guilt, death and eternity, and moved towards her favourite texts, John 3: 3, 5: 24, 6: 37; Acts 16: 31. She took special pleasure in quoting, "The blood of Jesus Christ, his Son, cleanseth us from all sin," 1 John 1: 7. Some of the popularity of her tracts was no doubt due to the fact that she was herself always ready to pass on a tract to those whom she met. Her husband tells us that "scarcely ever did she get into a railway carriage, or into an omnibus, but she presently offered tracts to those within reach, and endeavoured to begin a conversation with some on spiritual things; the free grace of God in Christ, and the sufficiency of the blood of Jesus to cleanse from all sin, being her ordinary topics. She thus acquired an ever-increasing acquaintance with the human heart, and with the various devices employed by Satan to keep sinners from Christ; and thus obtained, by the help of the Holy Spirit, power to bring the Word to bear on such and similar cases."[8] "She possessed a remarkable power of obtaining the confidence of strangers. It was quite a common incident for a chance companion in an omnibus to open up to her the history of her life, and this though she was by no means communicative of her own private affairs. Often has she come home and told me a story full of romantic passages which had been confided to her by some forlorn woman whom she had met laden with trouble. I believe it was largely owing to her great power of sympathy which was quick to read trouble and sorrow in another's countenance, and which then, by some gentle word of inquiry or condolence, opened the spring of grief so that it poured forth."[9]

Most of her tracts were published by the Weekly Tract Society of 62 Paternoster Row, the rest in a monthly issue of the *British Messenger* of Peter Drummond, Stirling, and other publishers. Then in 1864 Morgan & Chase published 54 of them along with six by her husband in one volume as *Narrative Tracts* by Mr and Mrs P H Gosse. It is estimated that seven millions of them were distributed and one at least was translated into French. She kept at writing them to the very last, as her husband related, "Nearly a hundred *British Messengers* the excellent publisher, Mr Drummond of Stirling, had been in the habit of sending her every month for distribution; and on this very last day [9th February, 1857], one of the servants was seated at a table by her bedside with heaps of Tracts and Messengers before her, folding and addressing each, under her dictation. It was her last act of earthly service."[10]

Notes

1   Quoted by Anna Shipton, from a letter by one who had known Emily for twenty years, in *Tell Jesus,* p 94

2   E[mily] B[owes]: *Hymns and Sacred Poems,* Bath, 1832.

3   Mrs Shipton recalls, "She was very slow to judge others, but very swift in judging herself," *Tell Jesus,* p 89.

4   E[mily] B[owes]: *Hymns and Sacred Poems,* Bath, 1834.

5   E[mily] B[owes]: *Hymns and Sacred Poems,* Bath, 1834.

6   Her son wrongly says in *Father and Son,* p 25, that his mother was "cold about foreign missions" see note 7 Chapter 4.

7   *Abraham and his Children,* p v.

8   P H Gosse, *A Memorial of the last days on earth of Emily Gosse,* London, 1857, p14f.

9   Ibidem p 24f.

10   Ibidem p 73.

Chapter 8 – Joys and Sorrows

We need to retrace our steps somewhat to examine the years which can without hesitation be described as Emily's finest. Her sympathetic spirit has been already remarked upon, and in 19th century England there was indeed plenty to call forth that sympathy. She made new friends easily, and cherished old friends too, by the deep personal interest she took in all her friends as well as in everyone else she met.

It was in the spring of 1841 that she was able to leave her governess post in Hove to live with her parents in Upper Clapton in London. It was in early June of that year that she paid a return visit to the rectory at Compton Beauchamp where she would have had plenty of news to exchange with all the Hawkins family. There was probably the added attraction of travelling all the way from Paddington to Uffington by the railway which had just been opened in 1840.[1] The whole Hawkins family, except John, was present on the census night, the sixth of June, 1841, from Elizabeth, now 24, to little Fanny, only a year old (John was still at Pembroke College, Oxford). It is likely that she stayed at least until the Friday of that week when they would be celebrating the forty-eighth birthday of the Revd John Hawkins. The family were still living in the rectory although Mr Hawkins had been presented to the living at Ramsbury, Wiltshire, the previous year. She would have seen the growth in her former charges and met for the first time, Fanny, the baby. There would have been plenty to relate about Hove and the five orphan girls who had been under her care there. The contrast between the orphans, well-off though they were, and the happy united family in their country home, would not have been lost on Emily.

Among her recently acquired friends was Hannah Newton, the aunt of Samuel Prideaux Tregelles (1813-1875), the eminent Greek New Testament scholar. As Hannah Abbott she had been born in 1798 and had married Benjamin Wills Newton (1807-1899) of Plymouth in 1832. Philip Gosse recalls that Emily had lived "in endeared intimacy"[2] with

Hannah Newton at Plymouth where they had discussed Mr Newton's *Thoughts on the Apocalypse* (1843). Emily may well have made the acquaintance of the Newtons when they visited Hackney some time after 1841, and so her visit to Plymouth would have been in 1843 or 1844. Since Hannah Newton was diagnosed with tuberculosis in 1842, and died of it in May 1846, Emily would have taken this opportunity to provide compassionate help.

Philip Gosse arrived back in London from Jamaica on the 6th August, 1846, and would soon have busied himself with the sorting out of all he had brought back with him and with his writing. In 1847 his 458 page work, *The Birds of Jamaica* was published, and, in 1848, his 370 page one *The Monuments of Ancient Egypt and their relation to the Word of God*, but it was not until the early autumn of the latter year that his and Emily's romance had blossomed. This seems to have resulted in a proposal of marriage from him after his visiting her parents' home on Sunday 17th September. He wrote in reply to a letter from her on Wednesday, 20th September, "I wish your dear honoured Mother to know the state of my affections for you as soon as possible," and "since Sunday evening you have been much in my heart both night and day. If what I desire be, as I think, of God, He will bring it to pass and make us happy in each other, and helpers of each other's joy."

A month later Philip wrote to his brother William, in Somerset, "In a few weeks I hope, if the Lord will, to be united in the dearest and tenderest bonds to one whom I dearly and tenderly love, and who is eminently worthy of being loved – possessing in a very high degree an elegant and cultivated mind, and a heart trained by many years of acquaintance with God, to subjection to His will. Her name is Emily Bowes; she is about my own age, and has passed a large portion of her life in the capacity of governess in the family of a clergyman; but has been for the past seven or eight years in communion with us who break bread simply at Hackney. So that our acquaintance has been of several years' duration, and mutual esteem has ripened into love. We have the fullest confidence that the Lord means to give us increasing blessing by our union, and we have His smile upon it. It is also happy to know that all our beloved Christian friends happily approve of it and sympathize with us without a dissentient voice."

On Christmas Day that year Philip wrote again to William: "Myself and my beloved wife most cordially thank you for your very kind wishes and congratulations. And it will give you pleasure, I know, to be told that your wishes are realized, and that I am happy, far happier than I was ever before in my life. I have a wife who is in every way worthy of being honoured and loved, who is in every way a help meet for me, and for whom I can never be sufficiently grateful to God."

"We were married at Tottenham at the chapel where Brethren worship on the 22nd November, the ceremony was performed by our brother, Mr Robert Howard of Tottenham, in presence of the Registrar. Mrs Morgan was present and many of our Christian friends from Hackney, who with us had partaken of the elegant hospitality of our friends, Mr and Mrs Howard, at breakfast." The couple returned to Philip's home at 13 Trafalgar Terrace, Kingsland, where they would quickly learn the realities of being united in marriage.

As Emily would be forty-three on the 10th November, 1849, in the autumn of that year, a difficult confinement could be expected for a first pregnancy; however, on 21st September she was safely delivered of a son, Edmund William. Seven weeks later she recorded in her diary, "He was born at noon, September 21, Friday, but in consequence of never taking the breast, and my being weak and in need of rest, he slept first with nurse Yorke till October 9, and then with Mrs Thompson till October 20 – and on Sunday October 21st he first slept with me, and I found that he woke at 11, at 2, and at 5 for food, after which he would sleep no more, but required nursing the rest of the morning."

"We have given him to the Lord, and we trust He will early manifest him to be His own, if he grow up. And if the Lord take him early we will not doubt that he is taken to Himself. Only if it please the Lord to take him, I do trust we will be spared seeing him suffer in lingering illness and much pain. But in this, as in all things, His will is better than we can choose. Whether his life be prolonged or not, it has already been a blessing to us and to the saints – in bringing us to much prayer, and bringing us into varied need and some trial." "His first visit to Clapton was on Sunday October 28; his grandmamma [Bowes] was delighted with him and he behaved very well, not crying all the day." "This day [Sunday, 4th November] went to the Room for the first time after my confinement.

Mr Balfour prayed for us and for our child that he may be the Lord's." Emily now breaks into prayer. "May I be blessed in training my little one. May I commend myself to my dear Henry in my efforts, and succeed and be helped by his wisdom, his prayers, his sympathy, and his assistance. May I never lose my temper with my child – never punish him hastily, nor in proportion to my own inconvenience; not for my pleasure, but for his profit [Hebrews 12: 10]. May I not spoil him nor spare for his crying."

As winter approached the baby became the centre of attention. On 29th October he was taken out into the garden by Mrs Thompson, and on 10th and 22nd November [her own birthday and her wedding anniversary respectively] Emily brought him to Upper Clapton to visit his grandparents again. She wrote in her diary afterwards, "I have made up my mind to give myself up to baby for the winter and accept no invitations – to go when I can to the Sunday morning meetings, and to see my Mother." Three weeks later she wrote, "Since I wrote last, baby has made considerable progress. He grows tall and plump, and fairer and larger. He begins to take notice of persons, and smiles and even laughs. For the last ten days I have had nearly the entire charge of him. On the 16th instant our Mother [Mrs Hannah Gosse] left us and we had a new servant. Kate is very fond of him, and he is very good when with her. He discovered the moon last night and watched it very attentively. Since his grandmamma left I have washed and dressed him night and morning. The process takes me about three quarters of an hour, and nearly as much longer to rearrange everything afterwards; at least it took that time tonight."

With the winter past, baby's first Spring was all full of wonder, but on 10th June, 1850 Emily's father died. William Bowes had been shattered by the financial collapse in 1814, but with some determination had set about building things up again. They had set up house in 1831 and lived modestly in Upper Clapton until at the age of 78 he passed away and was buried at Old St Mary's churchyard, Stoke Newington on 14th June. A fortnight or so later, word reached Emily that her aunt, Sarah Bowes, was dangerously ill in Leamington Priors.

This aunt of hers had been born in Boston, in Massachusetts, on 31st January, 1773, but her mother had died when she was just over fifteen months old. Her widowed father having taken the British side in 1776, she was brought to England by him with her brother, at the evacuation on 17th March when she was only three years old. Having been success-ful in business, her father had left her comfortably off when he died in 1805, but she had remained unmarried. On Sunday evening 30th June, Emily wrote in her diary, "Going to L tomorrow with E [her brother Edmund] to see my aunt. Lord, prosper my journey. May I find her alive. May I have access to her. May I find her in possession of her faculties. May I have opportunity of setting Jesus before her. May she receive Him soon, at the last hour, as a child. Lord, save her soul... May my journey not be in vain. Keep us from covetousness, from the love of money, from desiring what is not ours. May this money come to us or not as would be best for us, and may we be content with my appointment." Whether Em-ily arrived in time is not clear. Sarah Bowes died at Eden Cottage in Char-lotte Street in Leamington Priors on 1st July, and was buried in Warwick. On 17th July 1850, Edmund Elford Bowes was granted administration of her estate of £9000 at the Probate Office in London. At the beginning of August Emily returned to Leamington Priors for a week to clear the house and its effects, and part of the time she was helped by her brother. In due course the estate was dispersed and some of the proceeds were invested, at the recommendation of Philip Gosse's younger brother, in Cornish mining shares, but they collapsed. Between them Emily and the brothers lost about £2500 so that in an indirect way her prayers were answered.

And the next year, 1851, was to carry its share of sorrow too, for Em-ily's mother, Hannah, died on 14th January of that year at the age of 82. Her health had been deteriorating for some time and she had become quite lame. Her childhood had been disrupted by having to leave Boston when she was seven years old, and losing her father when she was eleven, and yet it was from her that Emily had imbibed her thirst for knowledge. Emily and her brothers greatly loved and respected her and it was an indi-cation of how accomplished she was that she taught them classics.[3] A headstone of four feet in height in the churchyard marks today where she and her husband were laid to rest. Then on the 1st of February fifty-three year old Mrs Elizabeth Hawkins of Wiltshire, Emily's loved former mistress, died, too.

Throughout all this time, between 1849 and 1851, Philip Gosse had worked diligently at his writing and published eight titles. All this, how-ever, was too much for him and in January 1852 his doctor urged him to leave London for a spell so that he might recuperate. And so, for the next four years the Gosses spent most of their time at the coast. On 27th January, 1852 they left London for St Marychurch near Torquay, and in April they moved to Ilfracombe in north Devon where they stayed until November. In 1853 they were from April to December in Weymouth, and then in 1854 they spent six weeks in Tenby, South Wales, from 22nd June to 18th August. In the following year they stayed again in Weymouth from 20th March to 13th May and at Ilfracombe from July to early September. Nevertheless, these were busy times for Philip Gosse, devoted to collecting samples from the shore, but for Emily and little Edmund there was a tonic in the sea air, while she also found fresh material for her Gospel tracts in her contacts with people she met there.

Anna Shipton relates an incident which lets us see the qualities of Emily which impressed her most. She had been invited to London to spend a few days with her, but on her first night Anna was restless and unable to sleep. "The morning had hardly broken when she quietly opened my door, and brought to my side the breakfast which her thoughtful care had provided. She had lighted the fire in her husband's study, to avoid disturbing the servants; she had heard my restlessness, and was ever on the watch to serve. When I told her how grieved I was for her to rise to do this, her reply was like herself. 'Supposing that yesterday Jesus had rested in your lodgings on His way to Jerusalem, weary with His journey, and you knew He had been watching all night, should you have thought it any hardship to rise an hour or two earlier than usual to give Him refreshment? Jesus could not come Himself, He sent you; and He says to me, "Inasmuch as you have done it unto her, you have done it unto Me."'"[4] [Matthew 25: 40].

On her birthday, 10th November in 1855, Emily wrote in her diary, "I have completed my forty-ninth year of life and the seventh of my married life. Lord, forgive the sins of the past, and help me to be faithful in future. May this be a year of much blessing, a year of Jubilee [Leviticus 25]. May I be kept lowly, trusting, loving. May I have more blessing than all former years combined. May I be happier as a wife, mother, sister, writer, mistress, friend. May my beloved husband and myself walk uninterruptedly in grace, love, faith and communion with Thee and each other. May he be much blessed in preaching and teaching Thy word. May he be kept from the love of earthly things, and live more and more in heavenly things. May I be more successful as a mother. May my sweet boy be obedient, truthful, subject and humble. Take away his faults and let us have Scriptural grounds for believing that he is saved, and then may he grow continually."

Her husband quoted part of the above in his *Memorial* and continued, "I believe my beloved's prayer was fully answered, and that this was the best year of her life; but through much tribulation, through great agony of body, was her spirit made ripe for glory. In a great measure laid aside from her favourite employment, the writing of Gospel tracts, she was called to glorify Him whom she loved, by a patient endurance of His will, by bearing the most torturing pain. But 'He doeth all things well;' and this she knew and loved to testify. Almost immediately after the supplications above mentioned were recorded on high, the gracious answer began to be given. At first it came only in joy. The firstfruit was a very blessed revival of my own soul through some words which she spoke to me. And then there followed what she had reason to judge the sound conversion to God of three young persons within a few weeks, by the instrumentality of her own conversations with them. Others were impressed and appeared convinced of their sinful state, though she had no means of knowing any further result. Moreover, before the year was completed, at least two instances were brought to her knowledge of her Gospel tracts having been blessed to the decided conversion of souls. And the grace of the Lord was displayed to her also, in causing these testimonies to the blood of Christ, the fruits of her pen, to be spread very widely, even to the most distant parts of the globe, the results of which will be fully known when the harvest of this sowing time will be gathered in."[5] "During the twelve-month between November 1855, and November 1856, seventeen Gospel tracts of hers were published by the Weekly Tract Society, in addition to fourteen of hers already in their catalogue; and five more were printed between the latter date and her death, which have been published posthumously..."[6]

It would seem only fitting to close this chapter of joys and sorrows with one further quotation from Philip Gosse's *Memorial*. "Hitherto we had known nothing but ease and happiness in the seven years of our married life; and it was not infrequently remarked by us to each other, that the common lot, the badge of discipleship, seemed to be unknown to us. My beloved very frequently observed to me, and that especially during the year or two that preceded her mortal illness, 'How very happy we are! surely this cannot last!' Alas, it was soon to end... Slightly alarmed at the lump in her breast, my dearest Emily took the first opportunity of showing it to her tried friend, Miss Stacey, of Tottenham, who immediately accompanied her to Dr Laseron. She returned to me in the afternoon, met me with her usual quiet smile, and with unbroken calmness told me that he pronounced it cancer!"[7]

Notes

1   N Hammond: *Rural Life in the Vale of the White Horse, 1780-1814*, Reading, 1974, p 118.

2   P H Gosse: *A Memorial. ..* London, 1857, p 55.

3   Anna Shipton: *Tell Jesus,* p 92.

4   Ibidem, p36f.

5   P H Gosse: *A Memorial. ..*London, 1857, p 2.

6   Ibidem, p2ff.

7   Ibidem, p4ff.

▌Chapter 9 – "A sinner so signally loved"

In a notebook which Emily used to copy extracts she took from various prose and poetic writings, the last entry was one contributed by Margaret Wathen, the wife of William Yapp, Christian bookseller of Hereford and London. It was a poem, later adapted as a hymn, written by Anna Letitia Waring (1823-1910), with the title, *My Times are in Thy Hand*.

Father, I know that all my life
  Is portioned out for me,
And the changes that will surely come
  I do not fear to see,
But I ask thee for a present mind
  Intent on pleasing thee.

I ask thee for a thoughtful love
  Through constant watching wise,
To meet the glad with cheerful smile,
  And to wipe the weeping eyes,
And a heart at leisure from itself
  To soothe and sympathise.

I would not have the restless will
  That hurries to and fro,
Seeking for some great thing to do,
  Or secret thing to know;
I would be dealt with as a child
  And guided where to go.

So I ask thee for the daily strength,
  To none that ask denied,
And a mind to bless with outward life
  While keeping at thy side,
Content to fill a little space
  So that thou art glorified.

> In a service that thy love appoints
>   There are no bonds for me,
> For my secret heart is taught the truth
>   That makes thy children free,
> And a life of self-renouncing love
>   Is a life of liberty.

Such could be an accurate description of Emily's own outlook on living for her Lord here, most evidently in the last eight months of her life.

On the day after Emily had seen Dr Edward Laseron she consulted Dr Henry Salter, FRCP, who, in turn, recommended the eminent Sir James Paget (1814-1899) who was regarded as "the first authority on cancer" in London at that time. They both agreed with Dr Laseron's diagnosis and advised surgery. Dr Salter, the son of Philip Gosse's cousin, had heard of an American doctor, Jesse Weedon Fell,[1] who was inviting professional visitors to his clinic where he was demonstrating his "new cure" for cancer. Dr Salter accordingly attended on one of the open days and reported back to Philip and Emily who agreed to consult Dr Fell themselves. When they did, they were shown photographs of many patients at various stages of treatment, were given statistics of the success rate, and were assured that the pain experienced "was not worth speaking of."[2]

The anxious couple were cast upon the Lord for guidance with regard to the critical decision they had to take. They had agreed between themselves that no treatment should be undertaken unless they were united in deciding upon it. That agreement was for Dr Fell's clinic and, accordingly, Emily began the course on the 12th May, 1856. To travel to the clinic from their home in Huntingdon Street involved taking an omnibus from Barnsbury Park to Ludgate Hill or St Paul's, and another from there to Pimlico, involving having to travel for more than an hour and a half. These fatiguing journeys had to be undertaken three times a week. Philip Gosse recorded that these journeys, however, "opened up to her, what she greatly loved and valued, opportunities of serving her Lord in testimony, both by distribution of Gospel tracts, and by conversation with strangers."[3]

The treatment consisted of two ointments applied to the breast on alternate visits. One of these ointments contained lead iodide, and the other, zinc oxide mixed with an extract from a plant, *Sanguinaria Cana-densis*. Her husband wrote, "One of the unguents employed was attended with pain, presently causing a gnawing or aching in the breast which at times was scarcely supportable."[4] And, on the "painlessness of the treatment, in which to judge from what my beloved Emily subsequently underwent, as well as others who were treated coetaneously [at the same time] with her; I believe we were greatly deceived."[5]

On some of these journeys certain of her close friends accompanied her to the clinic and two of them have left their impressions of the experience. Mrs Hislop wrote, "On one occasion I accompanied her to Dr F's; and, while waiting, she spoke, as was her wont, to most of those seated around the room. She came at length to a poor man, who appeared to be in a very suffering state, and asked him about his hope for eternity. He replied to the effect that he hoped that he should do pretty well. She walked a few paces from him, and then returning, solemnly said, 'There is but one way to be saved; – the blood of Jesus Christ, God's Son, cleanseth from all sin.' She added a few more words to the same effect; but what affected and delighted me was that, in her fervour, she no longer addressed that man in particular, but there she stood as God's witness, and in tones that all in that room might, and I believe, did hear (although, perhaps, herself unconscious of it), proclaimed the blessed tidings of salvation."[6]

Mrs Shipton gave this account of her visit, "Among these poor stricken ones Emily Gosse moved as a ministering angel. Great was the fatigue she endured in these journeys, to and fro, but she only dwelt on the opportunities they afforded her of telling to poor sinners the love of Jesus, or from time to time of grasping the hand of some fellow-pilgrim by the way. The omnibus and the waiting-room were alike her field of labour. That morning every one was very civil to us; receiving her tracts and Messengers with courtesy, and many read them. That happy morning is still fresh in my memory. I had Emily to my heart's content all to myself, and we spoke uninterruptedly of what was dearest to both of us – of Jesus, and his dealings with his people. A tedious case preceded our arrival, and we had long to wait. A young lady whom she expected to meet her there failed in her appointment and this gave us the opportunity of a prolonged conversation. We both said, 'It is good to be here!' When I remarked that it was the only unbroken interview I had ever had with her, she smiled her bright arch smile, and immediately directed my attention to the young friend whom she had expected, and who was now entering the room. Still, I was so full of thankfulness for this happy hour of communion in our beloved Lord, that I did not murmur. Other patients soon followed, and my interest was absorbed in watching Emily's gentle greetings to some that she had met before, and to others – whose anxious or listless countenances she was scanning in deep sympathy. And again and again she recurred to the love of the Lord in opening out to her these opportunities of serving Him, and that among souls which she could not otherwise have reached."[7]

The treatment continued through May to August when another difficulty arose. Philip Gosse had committed himself to going to Tenby in South Wales for five weeks from 29th August. During that time he had arranged to conduct classes for the "out of door study of marine natural history," and give four addresses on Bible Prophecy on Sunday evenings in the Assembly Room. Dr Fell, however, consented to Emily travelling and provided a supply of the ointments, instructing her on their application. The *Tenby Observer* of 12th September reported, "Last week we announced the arrival of a well known friend of Tenby, Philip Gosse. It was a sight that went to our hearts, to see the hero, whose locks our enthusiasm had silvered in our dreams, descend the side of the vessel. In his right hand he bore a basket (pardon the vulgar term), an emblem of himself, being full of all things curious, and so he was borne to the shore. We understand Philip Gosse has been very successful in drawing around him a circle of admirers of nature's charms, before whose eyes he daily unfolds the chart of wisdom." Emily and Philip had been in Tenby in happier circumstances in the summer of 1854 and Philip had written an account of that visit in a 428 page volume which was published in March, 1856, entitled *Tenby, a seaside holiday*. In a lengthy review of it in *The British Quarterly Review*, the reviewer conjectures on what Tenby should do to honour Philip Gosse in return for his service to them, and suggests the erection of a silver plated aquarium and free accommodation on future visits!

It must have been an exacting journey for Emily as the train took them only to Narberth station, and the remaining nine miles had to be covered by a horse-drawn coach. They stayed at Cambrian Guest House in Tenby close to the beach, but, during their stay, as Philip Gosse recalled, Emily's discomfort was acute. "Our sojourn at Tenby continued from the 29th of August to the 2nd of October. During the first three weeks my Emily was ill with general weakness and headache and afterwards the use of the ointment furnished by Dr F produced such intense aching and "drawing" pain in the tumour, that altogether it was a time of much suffering. There were few days, however, in which she was not to be seen, according to her custom, on the sand, offering her tracts to the visitors, conversing with a bathing-woman, or sitting on the rocks by the side of some nursing governess, or mother, sowing in her own effective way, the good seed of the kingdom."[8] He added a touching account of how they took their leave on Sunday evening, 28th September, of the little group of Christians with whom they had fellowshipped. "Before we left, they gathered together to commend us to the Lord's care and my beloved thought it well that I should mention to them, as so gathered, the nature of her disease, which hitherto they had not known. They received the tidings with simple but most true-hearted sympathy; and the prayers which one after another of the little company, with many tears, went up to God for us both, were something to be treasured up in my memory as long as I remain in the body, as I am sure they are treasured up in the memory of Jesus, to be brought out unto praise and honour and glory at his appearing."[9]

Retracing their journey home to London no time was lost in consulting Dr Fell again, who now advised the removal of the tumour. To facilitate this, on 10th November, lodgings were taken for Emily and Edmund in Pimlico close to the clinic. On the next day the process of extraction surgically began and was continued for twelve days. As Philip recalled, "Her sleep was greatly disturbed by the pain. In health she had been accustomed to sleep well, and had been generally able to forget herself in a few moments after lying down, whether by day or night. But from the commencement of the extraction to her departure, it was a rare thing with her to be unconscious more than half an hour at a time, and a large portion of every night was passed in the wakefulness of pain. From the first she was unable to lie down, so that the repose she took was in a semi-recumbent position, propped up by pillows. The progress of the operation was attended by considerable aching, and loss of muscular power in the left arm, which prevented her from reclining at all on that side; hence she was reduced to using the half-sitting posture, varied occasionally by a slight leaning over to the right side."[10] This continued until

Sunday, 23rd November when the tumour became detached, much to Emily's relief.

If their hopes were raised by the removal of the tumour, they were soon to be dashed; Dr Fell decided to begin the removal process all over again on another tumour portion. Emily's strength was being reduced considerably, but her husband recalled that "amidst all the sighs and moans wrung from her in the course of this sore affliction, I never heard her utter a single murmuring word; not an expression, not a look that intimated a doubt of the loving-kindness of the Lord. She delighted to dwell on his goodness; and it was often when others less instructed in God's school, might have failed to trace it, peculiarly manifested to her, because of her quick understanding in the fear of the Lord. 'How merciful it is of the Lord that –' was so frequent a commencement of her sentences, as to be recognised as quite characteristic by those who were intimate with her."[11]

On Wednesday, 17th December, the second portion of the tumour, about the size of an egg, detached itself from the outer side of the breast. However, pimples were forming under the arm,[12] and on Monday, 22nd December, Dr Fell intimated that he would need to take out another piece under the arm and then treat the inner side of the breast. At this point Emily asked, "But how do you account for this spreading of the disease beyond the part you have all along been dealing with?" To this the doctor replied, "Oh, 'tis in your blood." Philip, who was commuting between their home and Pimlico, was told what the doctor had said that afternoon, and was again faced with the problem of deciding with Emily on the next step. Would they pursue this painful treatment with so little hope now of success, or turn to another treatment altogether? Their decision was for the latter. That same afternoon they returned to their home in Huntingdon Street resolved to take up homeopathic treatment.

Emily had been constrained by Dr Fell to take opiates at night, but now without them she could only sleep for short spells. This affliction was, however, greatly eased by the frequent repetition of Augustus Toplady's *Hymn of Sleep.*

What though my frail eyelids refuse
    Continual watchings to keep,
And, punctual as midnight renews,
    Demand the refreshment of sleep:
A Sovereign Protector I have
    Unseen, yet for ever at hand:
Unchangeably faithful to save,
    Almighty to rule and command.

Kind Author and Ground of my hope,
    Thee, thee for my God I avow;
My glad Ebenezer set up,
    And own Thou hast helped me till now.
I muse on the years that are past,
    Wherein my defence Thou hast proved,
Nor wilt Thou relinquish at last,
    A sinner so signally loved.

Often, as she lay with closed eyes, she would repeat that last line giving special emphasis to the word "signally."

Dr John Epps, the noted homeopath, was called in and in addition to the cancer, he warned of a diseased condition of the lungs. However, he declared himself unable to reverse these conditions, but did tell them that he hoped to relieve the suffering, and this was substantially effected. On her twenty-fifth birthday Emily had written,

Though if this year should be my last,
If death arrive ere this be past,
Though suddenly Thou stop my breath,
Or, by a painful, lingering death;
None of these things move me; I can flee
By faith to him who died for me,
Secure I am, though globes decay,
And earthly kingdoms pass away.[13]

At the same period she had framed the prayer which was now being answered:

While in health I still remain
Fit me for a bed of pain!
Grant, O Lord, that I may learn
Suffering into good to turn.
Thus each hour of life, may I.
Be preparing, Lord, to die.[14]

Mrs Shipton described it fittingly, "At the word of the Lord, Emily had thankfully walked in the sunshiny paths, telling of Him whom to follow was her life's glad service; and now when He had laid her low – how low! – and put into her hand the cup mingled with myrrh, in place of the new wine, it was well also."[15] Emily had made her own assessment, "I feel, that be it much or little, I have finished my course. I have loved the Lord and his work; and my only thought, if He were to give me another twelve-month of life, would be that I might labour a little more for Him."[16]

58 Huntingdon Street

In the mercy of God, although the cancer had been becoming more virulent, thanks also to Dr Epp's treatment, there was little pain in the breast, and the progress of the disease seemed to have been in remission. Her cough, though, was what distressed her in the closing weeks. However, just as on a day at Pimlico when she was wearied and heated and Mrs Shipton had arrived and bathed her perspiring hands and arranged her pillows, so another mercy was shown her in Barnsbury, Philip's cousin, Mrs Ann Morgan of Bristol, arriving on Tuesday, 20th January, and taking on much of the nursing care for the next three weeks.

Those three weeks saw a steady decline in her powers, and they all knew that the end was near. To her husband, Emily said, "My beloved

Henry, Gladly would I remain, if such were the Lord's will, and be your companion for the rest of your pilgrimage."[17] Then, only a day or two before her passing, she said with a look of unutterable affection, "I love you, – better than on my wedding day, – better than when I was taken ill, – better than when I came home from Pimlico."[17] "She fell into a heavy doze, breathing stertorously with laborious heaving and with opened mouth. I lay down in the room, the maids still hanging over her. In about three quarters of an hour I resumed my place by her side; she was as when I left her, and they told me she had not uttered a word, except once, that she said, 'Papa!' The breathing was now feebler, with less of the rattling of the phlegm. Presently she again breathed the familiar word, 'Papa!' which was the last word she uttered on earth. Her eyes now became fixed, and she was evidently unconscious, in no way noticing anything we said or did, till, exactly at one o'clock, she breathed a long expiration, and ceased. I laid her dear head, which for an hour had been on my arm, on the pillow, closed her eyes, and, all kneeling round the bed, gave thanks to God, amidst sobs and tears, for her peaceful admission into her happy Home."[18]

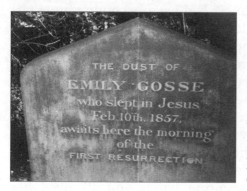

The funeral to Abney Park Cemetery took place on Friday, 13th February, 1857, in the presence of her relatives and of many of her Christian friends. The headstone, some five feet in height, is clearly legible to this day on grave number 17673 in Little Elm Walk,[19] the central path leading northwards from the cemetery chapel. It reads,

THE DUST OF
EMILY GOSSE
who slept in Jesus

Feb. 10th, 1857,
awaits here the morning
of the
FIRST RESURRECTION

Notes

1 For more about Dr Fell, see L R Croft, "Edmund Gosse and the 'New and Fantastic Cure' for Breast Cancer," in *Medical History,* 1994, no 38, p 143ff.

2 A large proportion of P H Gosse's *Memorial* has been reprinted in *Areté,* Winter 2001, with comments by radiotherapist, Professor Frank Ellis. I am indebted to Dr David Brady for drawing my attention to this article.

3 P H Gosse, A *Memorial*...p 14.

4 Ibidem, p 18.

5 Ibidem, p 7.

6 Ibidem, p 39.

7 Anna Shipton, *Tell Jesus*, p 58ff.

8 P H Gosse, A *Memorial*... p 20.

9 Ibidem, p 27.

10 Ibidem, p 30f.

11 Ibidem, p 35f.

12 Professor Ellis comments, "the appearance of pimples after the tumour had sloughed away would have warned a knowledgeable practitioner, even in those days, that the treatment had failed." *Areté,* p 86.

13 A Birthday Hymn, E[mily] B[owes]: *Hymns and Sacred Poems*, Bath, 1832.

14 Preparation, E[mily] B[owes]: *Hymns and Sacred Poems,* Bath, 1832.

15 Anna Shipton, *Tell Jesus,* p 98.

16 P H Gosse, A *Memorial*... p 68.

17 Ibidem, p 53.

18 Ibidem, p 78f.

19 Strangely, Edmund Gosse wrote in his biography of his father, p. 270, "My Mother lies in the remotest corner of Abney Park Cemetery", but the grave is three-quarter way along the Little Elm Walk, and far from any corner. Emily's brother, Edmund, appears to have been unable to attend the funeral, as William Gosse, on visiting his cousin, Mrs Morgan, recorded in his diary of 24th February that she had informed him "that Mr E Bowes was going about again."

▌Chapter 10 – Faith's Reward

It was in 1815, in Exmouth, as related earlier, that Emily became particularly aware of the spiritual influences in her life when she was given a copy of Legh Richmond's popular tract, *The Young Cottager*. She was greatly touched by its story and read it through again and again. Then, although in the main she attended the parish church with her family, she was taken by her mother several times to Glenorchy Chapel, where she was attracted by the plain preaching of the Revd Robert Winton. So were begun two practices which developed her spiritual life for years to come – reading of evangelical writings and listening to able preachers. In London in 1820 she had been greatly taken with the preaching of the Revd Edward Marsh, whose Bampton Lectures on *The Christian Doctrine of Sanctification* (1848) show something of the clarity with which he treated his subjects. As opportunity arose, she heard Daniel Wilson, Edward Irving, and Bishop Sumner in London and William Jay in Bath, and others in both and elsewhere.

While Emily was in Berkshire, her range of reading had grown to include Philip Henry, John Flavel, John Owen, John Howe, Legh Richmond, (especially his *Domestic Portraiture)*, T R Birks, M M Butt, Edward Bickersteth, Felix Neff, J F Oberlin and others, and so her grasp of Bible teaching was widening in scope and increasing in depth. In most of these there was an emphasis on holy living and personal witness to which Emily responded readily, and there was thus a building up of her Christian character.

And so, when, at the age of thirty-four, she came to live with her parents, she had already adopted regular habits of prayer and Bible study thus fitting her to be the effective witness to and compassionate helper of the needy to the end of her life. As Philip Gosse recalled, "Her character was eminently practical; she did not let her sympathy evaporate in sentimental speeches, but at once set about seeing what could be done. Her own purse strings were always loosely tied..."[1]

Mrs Shipton relates that Emily felt that she was learning from what she was seeing while lodging at Pimlico: "She told me of her sympathy for the poor and lonely that her lodgings had taught her, though it always seemed to me that she never lacked sympathy for any form of distress or suffering. 'How tenderly,' she said, 'we should think of the sick; the disorder of the sick-room, instead of exciting blame or disgust, should call forth our pity; perhaps, if they have anyone to care for them, even *they* may have many claims upon them, and this I have learned, with other things, here.' "[2]

During those years too, her faith had been developing and strengthening. It had been tested especially by the excruciating pain she suffered while under Dr Fell's treatment, and it had drawn forth much admiration from all who were close to her in her last three months, when her thoughts were turning more and more heavenward, as her husband so faithfully recorded, "to a friend who called a few days before her departure, she said, 'This will be the happiest year of my life: for I shall see Jesus!' "[3] "As she lay still, she said, 'I shall see his bright face, and shall shine in his brightness, and shall sing his praise in strains never uttered below!' "[4]

She could join with the apostle Paul when he said, "I am already being offered, and the time of my departure is come. I have fought the good fight, I have finished the course, I have kept the faith: henceforth there is laid up for me the crown of righteousness, which the Lord, the righteous judge, shall give to me at that day; and not only to me, but also to all them that have loved his appearing," II Timothy 4: 7, 8.

"Abney Park Cemetery was chosen as the place for the deposit of her dust, there to rest until the approaching manifestation of the sons of God. Then she shall rise to meet her Lord, renewed in resurrection power and beauty, changed into his likeness whose glory was precious to her soul."[5]

In conclusion, we can find that faith of hers fittingly described by her husband in the poem with which he closes his *Memorial*, and in which he shows how Emily had passed some of it on to himself.

"Himself hath done it," Isaiah 38: 15

"Himself hath done it" all. – O how these words
　　Should hush to silence every murmuring thought!
"Himself hath done it" – He who loves me best,
　　He who my soul with his own blood hath bought.

"Himself hath done it." – Can it then be aught
　　Than full of wisdom, full of tenderest love?
Not *one* unneeded sorrow will He send,
　　To teach this wandering heart no more to rove.

"Himself hath done it." – Yes, although severe
　　May seem the stroke, and bitter be the cup,
'Tis his own hand that holds it, and I know
　　He'll give me grace to drink it meekly up.

"Himself hath done it." O, no arm but his
　　Could e'er sustain beneath earth's dreary lot;
But while I know He's doing all things well,
　　My heart his loving-kindness questions not.

"Himself hath done it. " – He who's searched me
　　through,
　　Sees how I cleave to earth's ensnaring ties;
And so He breaks each reed on which my soul
　　Too much for happiness and joy relies.

"Himself hath done it. " – He would have me see
　　What broken cisterns human friends *must* prove;
That I may turn and quench my burning thirst
　　At his own fount of *ever-living* love.

"Himself hath done it. " – Then I fain would say,
　　"Thy will in *all* things evermore be done;"
E'en though that will remove whom best I love,
　　While Jesus lives I cannot be alone.

"Himself hath done it. " – Precious, precious words;
　　"Himself," my Father, Saviour, Brother, Friend;
Whose faithfulness no variation knows;
　　Who, having loved me, loves me to *the end*.

And when, in his eternal presence blest,
I at his feet my crown immortal cast,
I'll gladly own, with all his ransomed saints,
"Himself hath done it" – all, from first to last.

Notes

1   P H Gosse, A *Memorial.* p 39f.
2   Anna Shipton, *Tell Jesus,* p 100.
3   P H Gosse, A *Memorial.* p 63.
4   Ibidem, p 72.
5   Anna Shipton, *Tell Jesus,* p 110.

APPENDIX I
MOTHER AND SON

The serious reader today of *Father and Son* by Edmund Gosse may have to be reminded that, when the author was writing about his mother he was writing of one who had died fifty years earlier when he was only seven years of age. Would the passing of the years have preserved any but the vaguest memories, or would they have given him no more than an affectionate reverence for one he could hardly have known at all profoundly? From study now of his published and unpublished sources we can make an assessment of the accuracy of his portrayal of her in the book, and this in turn prompts further questions.

As has been shown in the main narrative, Edmund had allowed his imagination to provide a colourful picture of his maternal grandfather which bore little resemblance to fact. Would he be more careful in what he wrote about his mother? Let us look at just a few instances.

On page 5 of the 1961 edition, referring to both parents he avers, "For each there had been no poet later than Byron." Now just a glance at Emily's own notebook would have reminded him of Keble, Lyte, Moultrie and other poets, but did he refer to Byron with his tongue in cheek?

Another example is where he tells his readers, page 9f, "For over three years after their marriage neither of my parents left London for a single day, not being able to afford to travel." He had conveniently forgotten that Emily had twice in 1850 gone to Leamington for extended visits due to the death of her wealthy aunt, from whose estate she received a generous portion.

On pages 16 and 18, Edmund refers to his mother's "extreme dislike of teaching," but her own testimony is to the contrary as can be seen in about half a dozen of her poems. And a friend of hers of many years, quoted by Anna Shipton, says plainly that she was "fond of teaching", see Appendix II.

When Edmund deals with Emily's faith and its practice, again he shows an apparent ignorance. Any reader with a slight knowledge of religious life in the 18th century will feel a mixture of amusement and incredulity when he comes across the statement that his mother believed that he would grow up to be the Charles Wesley of his age or perhaps, she had the candour to admit, "merely the George Whitefield", page 25. Again, Edmund shows how out of touch he was with the evangelical faith of the Hackney group when he says, page 4, "By a process of selection, my Father and my Mother alike had gradually, without violence, found themselves shut outside all Protestant communions." The reverse was the case. It would seem that in the circle of Edmund's friends in London, he felt embarrassed by his mother's faith and so is somewhat dismissive of it.

Whilst in the area of personal description, let me give just two more examples.

On page 7 Edmund describes his mother as "possessed of a will like tempered steel." It may be a fine vivid phrase but it does not tally with the picture we have of her by others. Even Edmund himself conceded, page 30, "My Mother always deferred to my Father, and in his absence, spoke to me of him as if he were all-wise." Philip with his mature judgement told his brother that she had "a heart, trained by many years of acquaintance with God, to subjection to His will." And this is shown over and over again in her own diaries and poems.

Yet another example I must quote and it is the most extraordinary of all, page 5, "In this strange household the advent of a child was not welcomed, but was borne with resignation." The present writer has carefully sifted the correspondence, diaries and other writings and these are replete with evidence to the contrary.

The more I have researched the lives of the Gosses, the more apparent it has become to me that such statements by Edmund have to be treated with at least reservation where there is no corroborating evidence for them. But why did he so misrepresent his own Mother? Was James Hepburn not correct when he wrote in his Introduction to the 1974 edition of *Father and Son* published by Oxford University Press?

"In his Preface Gosse is high minded about his aim: he will not, he cannot trifle with his readers – 'the following narrative in all its parts, and so far as the punctilious attention of the writer has been able to keep

it so, is scrupulously true.' And yet Gosse was a man who was once pub-
licly embarrassed because of his errors in literary history, and whose
memory is pursued by the continual disclosure of others. Why should he
who was so inaccurate about Sir Philip Sidney, Donne, Gray and Swin-
burne be taken at face value about himself and his father unless it were
that he charmed his modern readers with their own prejudices?" It is my
own conviction that Edmund was so intent on composing his story in a
way that would regain the sympathy of his readers that he would distort
anything, including about himself and his mother, in the hope of
achieving it, for that reason as well as that of his feeling embarrassed by
the faith of his mother and so fails to recognise its worth.

APPENDIX II
EXTRACT FROM 'TELL JESUS'
(Pages 90 – 95)

One who had lived in sweet fellowship with her [Emily] eighteen years before I was blessed in knowing her, thus writes:-

I can truly say, that almost every recollection of my beloved friend is fragrant with the name of Jesus. She lived to serve and glorify Him; it was the one object of her life. I do not think I ever met with a person so single-eyed, or so consistent as a Christian; it was to me a continual memento of what we ought to be. Prayer was her strength, she took everything to Jesus; things pleasant or sad, perplexing or comforting, alike were imparted into his ever open ear. Oh, how often have we knelt together, and she taught me to seek for grace for others, as well as myself, at a throne of grace! She used to say, "We can never speak against anyone we have prayed for;" and "Let us ask the Lord," was her continual invitation. Her prayers were most simple and fervent, literally those of a loving child, in the greatest simplicity telling her Father everything, and owning his hand in everything. She used to say, nothing was too minute for Him to care for; and if she intended to go one way, and her plans were quite defeated, she could rejoice in the conviction that He was guiding her path, and this was happiness. She had great sympathy for those in trial, and sought by prayer to help them when in no other way she could. Though extremely cheerful, her heart responded instantly to the plea of sorrow, and by personal sympathy and prayer, she made the trials of others her own.

She was a most devoted daughter and sister. She told me her mother was a peculiarly clever woman, and that they were chiefly indebted to her for their love of knowledge. She taught them the classics, and Emily herself was quite a scholar. Latin and Greek she was familiar with; I feel uncertain about Hebrew. She was fond of teaching, and for some years, I know, she maintained her brother at the university by disinterested appropriation of her income to this object. They were a most united family.

Amongst the many precious reminiscences of our friendship, few things strike me more forcibly than what I would call her "family love." No matter whether rich or poor, learned or unlearned, agreeable or disagreeable, if she discovered in them the lineaments of her blessed Saviour, she was irresistibly attracted to them, and sought in every way to get good, or to do good.

Her self-denying efforts were unwearied in cases of emergency or distress, and no amount of disappointment or personal discomfort would change her purpose. Sometimes, when surprise was expressed that she was not discouraged, she would say, "We are all clay in the hands of the great Potter. He knows how to accomplish his purpose of making us vessels of honour [Romans 9: 21]; and as I must meet them in the glory and admire them then, I had better begin now to try what there is to like." Thus would she check a detracting spirit in others, by her example as well as her words, and lead the thoughts of her companions to that coming day, when Jesus Christ will own every instance of such service as done to Himself.

I have often thought the "inasmuch" [Matthew 25: 40] richly belonged to her. Do you remember her happy cheerfulness, which made her such a bright home companion, never gloomy, always buoyant for the occasion?

Those who knew her best loved her most, and were sure of her sympathy for joy or sorrow. Yet it is only right to state, lest some who slightly knew her should consider her character overdrawn, that a certain *brusquerie* of manner, and a want of completeness in the minor etiquette of society, often did great injustice to the real refinement of heart and mind which she eminently possessed.

After her marriage I saw much less of her: but still learnt by her example the value of God's Word, its practical power to meet every circumstance of life. It was a great change to one who had been always at liberty to visit and care for others, to fulfil literally the apostle's injunction, to be a "keeper at home," to "submit herself to her husband as to the Lord;" but she owned the duty as imparted from on high, and sought for the needed grace to "adorn the doctrine." She daily sought to "reverence her husband," and to merge all her tastes and wishes in his; so that she truly became a meet helper to him, and they walked together "as heirs of the grace of life." She greatly dreaded anything that should "hinder their prayers;" for union in Jesus was her aim in everything. Her sphere of service from this time was changed; but still how useful! What she did will only be known when the secrets of all hearts will be revealed; her tracts prove much. I believe few, if any, knew that they (Mr G and herself) mainly supported a missionary to the poor, and she herself told me that most of the striking anecdotes related in her tracts came under their notice through his visitations; others occurred to herself, and all were true. Dear Emily! I love to think of her, and owe much, very much to her; for our most intimate intercourse was ever at the mercy-seat. The last time she was here seems but a few weeks since, so vividly is it before my mental eye. She had to consult a physician, and told me, for the first time, what were her own fears, and his confirmation. Oh, how rapidly from that day she faded! it is difficult not to repeat, whenever I think of her, "Let me not fall into the hands of man, but into the hands of God." It was a fiery ordeal she endured during her last weeks on earth; but never can I forget her patience, submission, and peace: truly she realized the promise of "perfect peace" to them that wait upon Him. I only saw her three or four times; she seemed cut down in the vigour of life; but doubtless her work was done. I can always feel as regards her, how truly "blessed are the dead that die in the Lord; they rest from their labours, and their works do follow them." [Revelation 14: 13]

APPENDIX III

[Appendix III to VIII are samples of Emily's articles in periodicals and her Gospel Tracts.]

IS CHRIST WILLING?

In one of the suburbs of London lived, some years ago, a young servant girl whom I will call Eliza G–. She had continued up to her twentieth year indifferent to the value of her immortal soul, and concerned only for the things of this fleeting life, when one Lord's Day afternoon, having been permitted by her mistress to attend a place of worship, she heard a sermon which made her feel herself a lost sinner.

This was no transient emotion, but one that bowed her to the very earth; and in vain she sought relief by prayer and reading the Word, and by conversation with Christians. She feared to go to sleep at night, lest she should awake in hell; and though she was told to trust in the blood of Jesus, she felt so guilty she could not believe she would be forgiven.

Among her friends was a Christian young woman who was my servant, who told me of her sad case. I directed her to invite her young friend to come to see me the first time she had leave to go out. Not many days after, just as evening was drawing in, Eliza. G– ventured to pay me a visit. I was very glad to see her, and the following conversation, as nearly as I could take it down afterwards took place between us:-

"Walk in, Eliza; I was wishing to see you. I hear you are in distress of mind."

"Yes, indeed, ma'am; I am very unhappy, because I am such a sinner; I fear I shall never be saved: my sins are so great; they are innumerable."

"Do you think that Jesus is able to save you?"

"Yes; I know He is able."

"Then, do you think He is willing?"

"No, ! fear not; my sins are so very great."

"If I were a doctor, who could cure all complaints, it would not signify how bad the people were who came to me; the greater the disease the more would my skill be exhibited. I should not turn away those who had broken legs, and cure only those who had bad fingers. So all are alike to Jesus. He is able to cure all; He is willing to cure all who come to Him. He says, 'Whosoever will, let him take of the water of life freely.' So you see He is willing, if you are willing. He says, 'Him that cometh to me I will in no wise cast out.' Have you ever come to Him?"

"Yes; I am sure I have."

"Well then, why are you not rejoicing in Him? But perhaps you are waiting to feel happy in your own mind before you believe you are saved; many good people do."

"Yes, I do; that is just what I want to feel: then I should be happy."

"Suppose now, Eliza, you had been so wicked as to rob your master, and you came to me, and said, 'I have robbed my master, and lost or spent the money. I shall be found out and imprisoned. I am very sorry for my sin, but I can do nothing: can you save me?' I might reply, 'Eliza, you have destroyed yourself, but I will be your friend. I will refund the money, and save you from destruction; leave it all to me.' How should you feel?"

"Oh! I should be quite at ease, if I knew you would pay it all."

"But instead of that, if you said, 'I know you are able to pay that money, but I cannot believe you are willing; the sum is too great. If I saw the money put back in my master's drawers, I should be better satisfied.' In that case I should not feel at all flattered by your confidence: I should know you did not believe me. Suppose, again, that a good man, much your superior in every way, wrote you a kind letter, saying, 'Eliza G–, I love you; I wish to make you my wife.' How would you receive the letter? Would you go about weeping and lamenting your fate, saying, 'I love this man: but he does not love me: he will never choose me for his wife, I am sure. I am so unworthy of him; I have acted so untruly to him; I am sure he will never forgive me.' If I saw you in this state, I would cry, 'Eliza, now, be a wise girl; believe this kind letter of one who truly loves you; and, instead of going about mourning all the day long, sit down at once and answer this kind letter. Tell your friend that though you feel yourself quite unworthy of such love as he has manifested towards you, yet you gladly accept it, and simply believe it; and that you are happy in the prospect held out to you. "Should you not act thus?"

"Yes; I ought to do so."

"Well, cannot you act thus towards the Lord Jesus? In his holy word He tells you of his love; and that if you accept it, you will be his eternally. All you have to do is to believe this, accept it and be happy,"

"I wish I could know this."

"Do you think it likely, Eliza, that you care more about your salvation than the Lord does? Do you think the lost sheep was more glad to be found than the shepherd was to find him? Was the piece of silver more glad to be picked up than the women to pick it up? Which rejoiced most, the poor prodigal son, or his father? Was it not his father who expressed all the joy?"

"I see where I have been wrong," said Eliza, "and I hope I shall understand better in future."

"Do not put off this till tomorrow, Eliza; take your unbelief to Jesus, and leave it; and be like Hannah, when she had been in the presence of the high priest. She believed that her petition was heard, and her countenance was no more sad."

After a little more conversation of the same kind. Eliza professed that she understood what I had said; and I felt comforted in the hope that, indeed, she did believe; and that what I had explained to her from the Word warranted the assurance that faith is all that is required. I asked her then to kneel down and join me in prayer for her; after which I let her go, and heard nothing of her for a fortnight.

At the end of this time again meeting my servant, she told her that she was a new creature: that she had been very happy ever since she saw me; and that she knew now that she believed on the Son of God, and that believing, she had life through his name.

Now I have recorded the simple arguments which the Lord blessed to the soul of this poor girl, knowing that there are thousands in her state; and hoping that the same words may be applied to some of these mournful ones, who are not wilfully rejecting Christ, but who, from want of knowledge of his free grace. dishonour Him by distrusting his mercy and love to poor sinners, if such should read this page, I say to you, dear friend, come to Jesus at once: come just as you are; wait not to be better; wait not to feel happier; wait not to get power over your sins; wait for nothing; come and welcome to Jesus Christ.

From *Gosse's Gospel Tracts* No.18.

APPENDIX IV
DYING BY PROXY

Among the officers in the French army, during the reign of Louis Philippe, was a young man, the husband of an English lady of my acquaintance, an especial favourite of his royal master, who always liked to see him among his royal guard, and to have him near his person: so that Captain P– found it very difficult to get leave of absence from his post of service.

It happened, however, on the occasion of some great public day, that a friend and fellow-officer of Captain P's was very desirous to see the show to the best advantage; and he begged his friend to let him take his place. Mons P was willing: the leave of the superior officer was gained: Mons P went home to spend a day with his wife and children: while his friend rode at the king's right hand, enjoying the best sight of the gay scene.

Many attempts, as is well known, were made by the discontented and disaffected among the subjects of the citizen king, to take away his life; and one of these attempts was made on the day we speak of. The king, however, as usual, remained unhurt; but one of the officers was killed by the assassin's bullet, and *that officer was the one who had sought and obtained the place of Captain P–.*

Whether this signal deliverance wrought any saving change in the heart of this young officer, I know not; but it was an escape which ought to have solemnized his mind, and led him to think where his soul would have been, had his friend not changed places with him that morning.

An incident not very dissimilar to this was narrated to me by one who better knew how to value the deliverance of which he had been the subject.

"Were you ever in battle?" I asked of a Christian man who had in his younger years served as a soldier.

"Never;" he replied. "After I was brought to know the Lord, I constantly prayed that I might not be called to shed the blood of my fellow-creatures; and though war broke out, I was seven years with my regiment in India, I never was. The heat of the climate and forced marches over burning sands, brought on temporary blindness; so that when the regiment was ordered to the Punjab, I was unable to proceed with it. They went into battle, and my front-rank man was cut in two by a chain-shot. So if I had not left the army when I did, I should not have been here to tell you my tale."

"This was a narrow escape!" I observed, as he told me the story.

"Yes!" he replied with emphasis: "Another man died in my stead!"

This was not the only occasion on which another man had died in the place of this old soldier; and to this circumstance, I doubt not, he alluded, when he used the emphatic words with which he finished. Long before this, God's only-begotten and well-beloved Son left his throne and court above, and came on a loving errand to this distant world, – that he might die in the stead of that poor man. Not for him *alone,* indeed, but really and actually for him, as if there had not been another soul contemplated in the substitution. And for *you,* too, dear reader, if you truly and from the heart accept and embrace Him as your proxy; you also may say with the utmost confidence, *"He died for me!"*

Let me briefly tell you how this was. The sin of Adam did not take God by surprise: He foresaw it all, and had provided for it, in a way which should meet the poor guilty condemned creature's need, and yet honour his own perfections. Perhaps you ask, "Why did not God forgive man, and pass over his sin, without any penalty, as I forgive my child when he offends me?" Do you do so when you have threatened punishment for any particular offence? do you pass over the offence without inflicting the punishment? You may possibly do so: for you are a fallible, sinful creature; and strict truth and holiness do not appear of the same consequence to you, as they do to God. But He had said that death should follow sin; and *it must,* or He must give up his glory as the Governor and Lawgiver.

To wink at the sin, then, was out of the question; the penalty of death alone could blot it out. But is it possible for another to bear it instead of the sinner?

Yes; God had reserved to Himself the right of accepting a substitute, if a fit one could be found, able and willing to suffer the doom that was due to the guilty.

Oh! what a solemn moment was that, when, in the counsels of heaven, the question was put, if any proxy could be found for guilty man. Angels held their peace: though their loving hearts pitied the sinner, not one of them could be found who would bear the penalty due to sin. For it was not the death of the body only, but the death of the soul; that is, the separation of it from the face of God, which is the uttermost misery. And if one of them had been willing, he would not have been able: he owed to God his own obedience and love; he had no life to give, for a creature's life is not his own but God's. The highest angel is only a servant; nothing that he has is his own.

But a voice was heard, – "Deliver him from going down to the pit: I have found a ransom. Lo! I come to do thy will, O God!" It was the voice of God the Son. He was free, owing no obedience to the law, for He was the Lawgiver. His life was his own; He had power to lay it down. His life was of immeasurable, of infinite value; and therefore competent to be put in the balance against the lives of all sinners, even if ten thousand times more than they are.

His offer was accepted: in the process of time He came down to earth; was made man; lived a life of spotless obedience, and then shed his precious blood as the substitute for sinners, – the innocent for the guilty.

God now makes free proclamation, that since his Son has died, no hindrance exists to any sinner's getting to heaven. It is now made to hinge on your being willing to accept the substitute: whosoever believeth on the Son hath everlasting life. There is no other condition than this of believing, that is, accepting, Jesus as having died for sin; no good works of yours are required for your salvation.

I knew a gentleman whose son enlisted as a private soldier. When his father heard of it, he sought him out, and with much entreaty begged him to give up his course. He offered to pay any expenses required to procure his discharge, or to purchase a substitute. But no, the poor deluded boy would not hear of such a thing. He would see the world; he would go to India with his regiment. To India he went; and there he remained in the ranks all his life. His poor father and mother soon died, grieving over their lost child; his brothers and sisters lacked all the comfort, protection, and help which they ought to have had from an elder brother's love; all the care and expense that had been lavished on his education, were thrown away: but, *as he had rejected the offered substitute,* what could be done for him?

So is it with you, my dear reader. if you reject Christ as your substitute, there is no help for you, but you must bear your own penalty in hell for ever!

From *Gosse's Gospel Tracts* No.20.

APPENDIX V
THE POWER OF THE WORD

A Christian man, travelling in North America, met with an intelligent countryman with whom he entered into conversation, and found that he was indeed a truly instructed and humble Christian.

"Under whose ministry were you converted?" said the gentleman.

"By that of the Rev George Whitefield," replied he.

"I did not think that George Whitefield was ever in these parts."

"Nor was he, sir; I never saw him in my life."

"I thought you said he was the means of your conversion."

"So he was. A neighbour of mine had business many miles from this, and one day while he was away he chanced to come up to a place where Mr Whitefield was preaching, and heard his discourse. When he returned, he was telling me all his adventures: and among the rest that he had heard the celebrated Mr Whitefield preach. As I was very anxious to know what his discourse was about, my neighbour told me all he could remember, enough to show me that I was a lost sinner, and that my only hope was to come to Christ for salvation. I did so, and I was saved in coming to Him. A happy man I have been since that day."

A somewhat similar anecdote is related of the Countess of Huntingdon. She was one day accosted by a poor man who told her that she had been the means of his conversion several years before.

"I have no recollection of ever having seen you, my friend," replied the Countess, regarding him attentively. "Probably not, my lady ," rejoined the poor man, "but perhaps your ladyship will remember having a new wall built round your garden, when you used to come out and speak to the workmen. I was one day standing outside the garden wall, and I overheard you talking to one of the men. That conversation was the saving of my soul."

In these instances we see how effectual is the smallest seed of the Word of God, when it falls on hearts made ready to receive it. How many who read this tract have heard over and over again that Jesus is "the way, the truth, and the life;" that none can come to the Father but through Him; and that those who come to Him He will in no wise cast out; nor is it a sufficient excuse to say that you have never lived where the gospel is truly preached. Many have been converted by reading God's Word, without any assistance from those who preach it.

A clergyman in Ireland, once meeting with a poor blind man, between ninety and a hundred years of age, addressed him by remarking that he was a very old man.

He answered, "Aye, sir;" and after a short pause said, "It is well for me that I have lived to be old;" adding, in a low tone, "but it was bad for Solomon."

The clergyman asked him what reason he had for saying that.

"If Solomon," replied he, " had died when he was young, he would have been considered one of the greatest men in the world; but if I had died when I was young, I should have gone to hell. Solomon lived to disgrace himself, but I lived to obtain eternal glory."

The clergyman asked him on what grounds he looked forward to obtain glory.

"Sir," said the blind man, "all my dependence for salvation is in the blood of Christ, shed for sinners like me."

"And how did you learn to know Christ, and to desire his salvation?"

"It was by the Holy Ghost," he replied, "that I came to the knowledge of divine things,"

"But," inquired the clergyman, "have you not heard some one speak or preach about these things?"

"No, sir; I never met with anybody who could tell me anything about my soul, or teach me the way to heaven,"

"Then," said the clergyman, "how came you by the knowledge you possess? and where did you learn the Scriptures you have alluded to?"

"Well, sir," he replied, "as I told you, I thought nothing about God, and knew nothing of the way to heaven, till about a year ago, when my sight left me, My blindness reminded me that I was growing near to my end, and I felt I was unprepared for death. I could not help thinking that I could best learn the way to heaven from God's own Word; and though, being blind, I could not read myself, even if I had ever learned, yet I have a little grandson who *can* read; so I purchased a Bible, and made the boy read to me constantly. Through reading the Scriptures the Lord opened my heart to see the truth. He made me feel his love in providing a way by which an old sinner like me could be saved."

Here the poor old man broke forth into many expressions of praise to his God and Saviour, who had done so great things for him.

Reader, has the Lord done such great things for you? – have you not had at least as great advantages as the poor man you have been reading of? You may not live within the sound of the preached gospel, but yet it may save you, even though repeated to you by those who have heard it. When the word of God lights on prepared ground, it does not require much labour from the human instrument who sows it.

If your heart is prepared to receive God's truth, you will be ready to accept it from a little tract or a little child. If you cannot read or go to hear the word yourself, will you try and get some one else to read it to you, like this blind beggar?

If you feel anything like a proper sense of the value of God's Word, you will not think it too much to deny yourself something in order to obtain it.

A poor aged widow, who could not read, was very desirous, like the blind Irishman, of hearing God's Word. She found out a little boy, a shepherd's son, living near her cottage, who could read. But the child, being fonder of play than of study, could not be persuaded to read to the old woman as often as she desired. She was too poor to pay him for coming so she determined to rise an hour earlier than before, to spin; and by these means earned an additional half-penny, with which she hired the little boy to read to her every morning.

But why should we thus value the word of God? Because it contains all we know of God and his will. By this word we learn that we are all lost sinners, that in Adam we all died, and in our own persons we have continually transgressed; that there is no hope for us, absolutely none, except in accepting God's offer of mercy. God says to us, "Thou hast destroyed thyself, but in me is thy help." God has helped us in sending his Son Jesus Christ to die for us: – He suffered for us, the Just for the unjust, to bring us to God, He died on the cross to bear our sins; He was buried; He rose again; – by this we know that God was satisfied with the sufferings He had endured for us. He ascended into heaven, where He intercedes for his people; and lastly, He has sent down his Holy Spirit to dwell in the hearts of all who believe; and *that* Spirit guides them into the understanding of the truth contained in the word, and helps them to love and obey it.

These things we learn from the Bible; let us, therefore, hear it, and read it. Be not persuaded by any man to neglect this blessed word, but read it, believe it, obey it. Then shall you be saved by it, for "faith cometh by hearing, and hearing by the word of God,"

From *Gosse's Gospel Tracts* No, 30.

APPENDIX VI
OLD BETTY

I have learned in whatsoever state I am, therewith to be content.
Phil iv. 11.

"Have you never heard the story of old Betty?" said I to a friend who was telling me some sad history of domestic discomfort. "No!"

"Then let me tell it you. The story was told me by a young lady whom I met at the seaside, and though I believe it has appeared in print, I know no other version of it but the one she told me:-

"Some years after I was converted," said Miss F, "it pleased the Lord to lay me aside from active occupation, and to confine me to a sick couch for full two years. The inactivity was grievous to me, and my constant prayer was for restoration to health, and power once more to go about visiting the sick and teaching the ignorant; when visited by kind Christian ministers and sympathizing friends, my constant request was that they would pray for my recovery, and that I might have faith to believe that the Lord would heal me. Still I grew no better.

About the end of the second year, I, one afternoon, received a visit from a minister unknown to me, who, in God's providence, was then visiting the place where I lived. He read and prayed with me, He sympathized with my sufferings, and listened to my troubles. I lamented to him my weak faith, which I felt assured was the cause of my continued weakness of body.

'Miss F,' replied the minister, 'have you never heard the story of Betty, the old match-seller?' I had not. 'Old Betty,' said he, 'was brought to the knowledge of Jesus in her old age and from the time of her conversion never thought she could do enough for Him who had loved her and washed her from her sins in his own blood. She went about doing good. She was ready to speak of her Lord and master to all she met. She would nurse the sick, visit the afflicted, beg for the poor and for the heathen, she would give to those poorer than herself portions of what the kindness of Christian friends bestowed on her. In short, she was always abounding in the work of the Lord.

'But in the midst of this happy course; she caught a violent cold and rheumatism, and was confined to her bed; there she lay day after day, and week after week, and, I believe, lay there till the Lord called her home. On her sickbed Betty was as happy as she had been in her active duties. She was much in prayer – she meditated on the good things she had learned, and on the good land to which she was hastening.

One day Betty was visited by an old friend, a minister, who had long known her. He was astonished to see his once active and useful old neighbour so happy in her bed, and he said to her, "I little expected to see you so patient; it must be a great trial to one of your active mind to lie here so long doing nothing." "Not at all, sir, not at all" said old Betty, "when I was well I used to hear the Lord say to me day by day, Betty, go here; Betty, go there; Betty, do this; Betty, do that, and I used to do it as well as I could; and now I hear Him say every day, Betty, lie still and cough".

Miss F told me this story as she heard it from her visitor, and she said it had a very strong effect on her mind. She began to think that it was self-will rather than faith that made her so anxious to get well again, and she humbled herself before God, begging for grace to bear his will, rather than seek her own. She became tranquil, happy, and contented on her sickbed, and almost immediately after, it pleased the Lord to restore her to health, and continue her in it, to the time when I met her."

E.G.

From Drummond's *Stirling Tracts,* First Series, No 201.

APPENDIX VII
LITTLE MARY

What would Jesus say?

Little Mary Groves was the child of very pious parents, and gave, from a very early age, strong evidences of the grace of God working in her heart. One night, when left alone with her brothers and a young relation, who was brought up with them, she became very angry on some trifling occasion, and her cousin said, "Mary, what would your mamma say?" She looked thoughtful, and turning to her cousin said, "What would Jesus say? Let us all kneel down and ask Jesus to forgive me." The four children knelt down, and she became, after prayer, quite good and happy.

At another time she said to her mamma, "I wish you would take the frills off my trousers, mamma." Mrs Groves replied, "No, my dear, it is not worthwhile to take them off, as they are there; I should not put them on any more." The child said, "Do take them off; because I love them so, I cannot help thinking of them." This showed how early she gained acquaintance with the natural vanity of the heart. She was a very lively child, and though the youngest in the family, quite took the lead with her brothers, but was wonderfully subject to her parents; and seemed ripening for her heavenly home, loving to talk about Jesus. Shortly before her death she said, "I am so thirsty." The servant took her toast and water; she refused it, saying, "Call mamma." When her mother came she said, "Mamma, they don't know what I mean; I want to drink the *blood* of Christ, and to eat His flesh." [John 6. 53ff.] She was not quite five years old when she died, and was early ripened for glory. She asked on the last day of her life to hear the twenty-third Psalm, and said she knew Jesus was her Shepherd, and would guide her through the valley of death.

Mary's mother taught all her children early to fear and love God. She did not live to see her sons grow up, but they were both converted while young, and are now serving the Lord as missionaries in India.

If we bring up our children for God, and set them a good example, of our little ones we may also hope to say, "Whether they live they live unto the Lord, and whether they die they die unto the Lord. Let us pray and labour, and patiently hope for in due season we shall reap if we faint not."

> [The dear friend who wrote this little paper for us is gone to Heaven since she sent it to us – *gone, and* MISSED. Ponder her words, young mother, that being dead she may yet speak to you and to your children. – Editor.]

E.G.

From *The Mother's Friend*, volume X (1857) pp 136, 137.

APPENDIX VIII
EARLY CONTROL
By the late lamented Mrs P H Gosse

"If you are too tired to read to me any more, mamma," said a little boy to his mother, who had been devoting the evening to his instruction and amusement, "lie down on the sofa, and I will lie by you; and please, mamma, tell me a story." "Well, then, Willie," said his mother, "listen to what I am going to tell you. Some years ago there lived a man called Benjamin Haydon. He was much thought of; had many friends and ad-mirers, and might have been rich and prosperous, and have enjoyed all that this world can give, but he had a very bad temper, and he never would give up his own will; so that he quarrelled with his best friends, rather than yield to them. Why was this? I am sorry to say he had been al-lowed to have his own way. When a boy, his father and mother never sub-dued his will, and never taught him to be humble and obedient to his superiors; and never obliged him to ask forgiveness when he had done wrong. This was the cause of his failure.

'O why did I not yield?' he exclaimed, on one occasion, when he had of-fended Sir George Beaumont, a gentleman of wealth, who had been a great friend to him. 'Why did I not yield? It was because my mind wanted the discipline of early training. I trace all the misfortunes of my life to this early and irremediable want – my will had not been curbed. Perhaps mine is a character on which all the parts would have harmonized, if my will had been broken early.' Doubtless there was fault on his side as well as on that of his parents. God's grace could have enabled him to humble himself, and to subdue his temper, even when he had become a man. We are never obliged to give way to pride and ill-humour; nevertheless you see by this story what a wicked thing it is for parents to indulge their chil-dren: they may call it love, but it is the greatest unkindness."

"And what became of him, mamma?" said little Willie. "At last he killed himself: at the foot of his easel. Oh, if his poor mother could have known what could have been the end of her indulgence, I think she would have thought it kinder to teach him to control his temper in his childhood."

"Had you any reason for telling me this sad story, mamma? Do you think I am like Mr Haydon?" said Willie. "No, my love; but you often wish to have your own way, and think me unkind if I contradict your wishes. I wish you to see what is the end of self-indulgence. I wish also to take a lesson from this story myself, for I fear I am sometimes too indulgent to you; and this is not true kindness. How should I feel if you grew up like Benjamin Haydon. and died like him? I should say, My poor boy is lost for ever, and that, perhaps, because I did not teach him to be subject and obedient when a child. So he grew up, passionate and self-willed, and killed himself because he could not have everything his own way. Let us ask God's grace, my dear child, that I may bring you up under proper control, and that you may submit willingly, even when you do not understand my object in controlling you."

E.G.

From *The Mother's Friend*, volume XI (1858) pp14-16.

APPENDIX IX
PUBLISHED PROSE WRITINGS

Abraham and his Children, Nisbet & Co, London.

The Christian Weekly News, 13th March, 1855.
    † How a rich seamstress became a poor heiress.

The Christian Weekly News, 27th March, 1855.
    † The Evening Adventure.

The Mothers' Friend, Ward & Co, London.
    † Volume VI   — Letters from the Nursery, No.6.
    † Volume VII   — A Page for Young Mothers – The Raw Apple.
                    — A Page for Young Mothers – More Raw Apples.
                    — The Delicate and Industrious Young Mother.
                    — The Delicate and Industrious Young Mother, No. II.
                    — A Lesson on Prayer .
    † Volume IX   — "I don't want to be naughty."
    † Volume X   — Little Mary.
                    — The Blind Irishman.
                    — The neglected child of godless parents.
    † Volume XI   — Early Control.

GOSPEL TRACTS, various publishers.
    † The Anonymous Letter.
    † The Bad Leg.
    † The Bathing Woman and the Visitor.
    † The Christian Soldier.
    † The College Friends.
    † The Consumptive Deathbed.
    † The Cure for Cholera.
    † "Do Open the Door."
    † The Drowning Sailor.
    † The Drunkard's Wife.
    † Dying by Proxy.
    † The Dying Peasant Lad.
    † The Dying Postman.
    † The Eleventh Hour.

† The Faithful Nurse.
† The Fall of the Rossberg.
† Fire! Fire!
† Freedom.
† The Good Physician.
† A Happy Family.
† A Home Welcome.
† "Is Christ Willing?"
† "I've no Time."
† John Clarke.
† John Clarke's Wife.
† Mary Kelly's Letter.
† The King and the Prince.
† The King of Hungary.
† The King's Daughter.
† Love.
† The New Forest.
† "Oh that Night."
† Old Betty.
† The Old Soldier's Widow.
† The Pass Ticket.
† The Pilgrim to St Patrick's Well.
† The Portuguese Convert.
† "Prepare to meet thy God."
† The Prize Fighter.
† The Prodigal.
† The Railway Lamp.
† The Railway Ticket.
† The Reapers.
† The Ruin and the Restoration.
† The Recruiting Sergeant.
† The Sabbath Trader.
† The Scattered Tracts.
† The Sceptical Traveller.
† The Sermon on the Bible.
† The Stage Coach Companions.
† The Suicide.
† The Teacher's Visit.
† Thomas Winter's Stray Sheep.
† Tom Fowler the Boatman.

† The Towing Net.
† "This is what I want."
† The Two Hospital Patients.
† The Two Maniacs.
† The Two Tenants.
† What is Believing?
† The Young Guardsman of the Alma.

Hymns and Sacred Poems

A Birthday Hymn

Another year is passed away,
Once more I reach my natal day;
Thee, God of life, once more I praise,
For peace and health and added days.

Thy guarding power protects my head,
Thy watchful care defends my bed,
Thy mighty hand upholds me still,
And saves me from each threatened ill.

Be thine the praise for all the love,
Which from thy hand I daily prove;
Still do thou, Lord, my steps attend
And be, as heretofore, my friend.

And if thou my petition hear,
And spare me yet another year,
Grant to my body and my soul,
Thy wonted care throughout the whole.

Let the events that shall befall
Unto my good contribute all;
Unto thy glory let them be,
For that must be the best for me.

Though if this year should be my last,
If death arrive ere this be past,
Though suddenly thou stop my breath,
Or by a painful lingering death;

None of these move me, I can flee
By faith to him who died for me;
Secure I am though globes decay,
And earthly kingdoms pass away.

For Jesus is not weak to save,
And him for my defence I have,
In him I'll trust in peace and woe,
My all in heaven, my heaven below.

Dear Saviour! while on earth I live,
Myself into thy care I give;
And when I die, O grant me grace,
To see with joy thy glorious face!

A Collect for Quinquagesima Sunday

Lord Jesus, who thy church hast taught,
That all our works and gifts are nought,
If charity, best grace of heaven,
Be not to crown each virtue given;

To us thy Holy Spirit send,
To us thy kind assistance lend,
O shed on us this lovely grace,
O make our hearts love's resting place.

Lord, give us kindly charity,
Sole bond of peace and amity,
For till it on our hearts be shed,
Before thee we are lost and dead.

Let such a love to us be given
As that which brought thy Son from Heaven;
Through him we one petition make,
O hear us, for our Saviour's sake.

A Collect for First Sunday in Advent

Almighty Father! give us grace,
The works of darkness hence to chase,
  And every thought of ill;
Arouse us from the dreams of night,
Array us with the arms of light,
  And mould us to thy will.

This grace unto thy people give,
While in this mortal state we live!
  And may we seek and find,
That path, Lord Jesus, trod by thee,
When in thy great humility,
  Thou visited'st mankind.

That in the great and glorious hour,
When thou shalt come again with power,
  To judge the quick and dead,
To life immortal we may rise,
Through thee who reignest in the skies,
  Our life, our light, our head!

A Collect for Second Sunday in Advent

Blessed Lord! who hast sent us the Scriptures of truth,
To cheer us in age, and direct us in youth,
Who, the whole word of life for our learning hast given,
As a lamp to direct us most surely to heaven;
So grant us to hear them, and read them, and learn,
So grant us their truths into practice to turn,
So grant, the soft balm of thy life-giving word,
May patience and comfort in trouble afford,
That we may embrace, and for ever hold fast,
The soul-cheering promise of glory at last;
That life-giving hope of pardon and heaven,
Which through the Lord Jesus, to sinners is given!

A Collect for Fourth Sunday in Advent

Raise up, we pray Thee, Lord, Thy power:
Arise! and blessings on us shower,
   And succour us with might!
Arise, and haste to our relief,
For we are sunk in sin and grief,
   And cannot walk aright.

The race Thou hast before us set,
Though sorely hindered oft and let,
   O give us help to run,
Thy bounteous grace and mercy show,
And evermore Thine aid bestow,
   Till we the prize have won.

In Jesu's name we pray Thee thus,
For his sake do thou favour us,
   And all we ask for, send,
To him, the Holy Ghost, and Thee
Great Father! praise and glory be,
   When earth and time shall end!

A Collect for the 21st Sunday After Trinity

We pray thee now, O Lord,
   To us thy chosen race,
Pardon of all our sins afford,
   And give us thine own peace.

May we be cleansed from sin,
   And with a quiet mind,
A life of virtue now begin,
   And thy assistance find.

These and all gifts beside,
   We ask for Jesus' sake,
Who lived to teach us, and who died,
   Our peace with thee to make.

A father's prayer

Show mercy unto me, and give,
    Father of all, I pray,
The grace so virtuously to live
That all my children may believe
    The holy things I say.

May all my words and actions tend,
    To form their souls for heaven;
Teach them with all their joys to blend
Sweet thoughts of thee their heavenly Friend,
    Who every joy has given.

In every care and grief, may I
    Teach them to suffer pain,
I'll in my sorrow ever fly,
To thee who can all need supply
    And give relief again.

And in the daily coming care,
    And fretful ills of life,
Teach them, through me, the need of prayer,
To soothe the temper, and prepare
    For keener scenes of strife.

Lord! when I for my children pray,
    I know not where to end.
O listen now to what I say,
Bless my beloved without delay,
    Be in their youth their Friend.

A hymn

To praise thee, my God, and my Lord,
    My heart is attuned once again!
Recalled by thy soul-moving word,
    I burst in two, error's strong chain.
I weep for the sin which I loved,
    When enthralled by the tempter's wild madness,
And thoughts of thy grace unimproved
    Fill my heart with penitent sadness.

Oh let me not ever again,
    Forget the deep anguish I felt,
When, fearing contrition was vain,
    I first in sad penitence knelt!
I thought I had wandered too far,
    To receive any hope in returning,
My spirit and flesh were at war,
    My heart in wild tumult was burning.

But kindly thy hand was stretched out,
    My spirit was hushed to a calm;
Thy promise dispelled every doubt,
    And healed my torn heart with its balm;
Now I weep – but my tears are more sweet,
    Than the sins which were once all my pleasure,
My joy is to lie at thy feet,
    Thy favour I count my sole treasure.

Oh grant that I never may now
    Forsake thee, my soul's chosen rest!
I'm bound by deep gratitude's vow,
    And bound by thy favours possessed;
It needs but that thou should'st impart
    Such grace that I never may leave thee,
Ne'er admit other gods in my heart,
    And never more wilfully grieve thee!

A hymn

What love I, as I love thy cause?
What fear I, as I fear thy laws?
What trust I, as thy plighted word?
On whom rely, but thee, O Lord?

I love thy cause, it doth include
Whatever earth contains of good;
All other themes, though learned they be,
Have little interest for me.

Thy laws I'll fear, by them abide,
And nothing need I fear beside;
For torment is in earthly fears,
But thine, the soul supports and cheers.

Thy Word I trust, for it is sure,
Its promises are all secure,
My title-deeds to every good,
Sealed with the kind testator's blood.

And shall I not rely on thee?
None else was e'er so true to me;
And ills, of body or of soul,
That weary me, on Christ I roll.

What should I love then, as thy cause?
What should I fear, if not thy laws?
Where place my trust, but in thy word?
On whom rely, but thee, O Lord?

A meditation

Sweet is the thought, that Jesus knows,
And feels for all his people's woes;
Whate'er their sorrow, fear, or pain,
To him he biddeth them complain,
And he will surely give relief,
Or patience to support their grief.

Sweet is the thought! for us he died,
For us were pierced his hands and side,
Through faith in his atoning blood
Our erring souls make peace with God;
He pardons and upbraideth not,
He deals as though he sin forgot.

Sweet is the thought, that Christ can see
My secret sins, yet pity me;
That though my daily falls he knows,
He still his tender love bestows,
And comforts and supports my soul,
And kindly doth my heart control.

Sweet is the thought, that Jesu's grace,
Is pledged my spirit's foes to chase,
That he his Spirit will impart,
To sanctify and cleanse my heart,
That he will perfect victory give,
And teach his servant how to live.

Sweet is the thought! how justly dear!
That soon shall end my trials here;
And they whose life by faith is led,
Who in the paths of virtue tread,
How great, their endless joy shall be!
O! grant, dear Lord, that joy to me!

A morning hymn

Now, O Lord, I quit my bed,
    Where peacefully I slept;
Thee I thank who watched my head,
Sweet dreams o'er my slumber shed,
    And from all evil kept.

In the watches of the night,
    I but on thee depend;
Now returns the cheerful light,
And still I need thy aid and might,
    My weakness to defend.

For when sunk in calm repose,
    All helpless though I be,
I but fear from outward foes; –
Now I also shrink from those,
    No eye but thine can see.

All the snares that Satan lays
   To captivate my heart,
Evil thoughts, and sinful ways,
Obstacles bad habits raise,
   Make me from good depart.

Then my God! be ever near,
   And guard my heart this day.
Make me every evil fear,
When I faint my spirit cheer,
   And be my guide, I pray!

A morning hymn

Lord, I have passed another night
   Protected by thy care,
And would begin the hours of light
   In thankfulness and prayer.

While many in this night have said,
   "Would God! that it were morn!"
While tossing on their fevered bed,
   Sad, helpless, and forlorn;

And others in the paths of crime,
   Dishonest and profane,
In deeds of darkness spent their time,
   Dishonouring thy name;

From sickness, fire, and murd'rous foes,
   I have been safely kept,
And freed from cares and vexing woes,
   In perfect peace I slept.

Then since from crime, from pain, from grief,
   That hast exempted me,
Grant to all sufferers quick relief,
   And turn their hearts to thee!

And may I, bless'd so much above
    Man's usual lot below,
Strive daily more to prize that love
    Whence all my blessings flow.

A mother's prayer

Look, Saviour, from thy throne above,
Upon the children of my love,
    For whom I daily pray,
Thou who hast given them life and breath,
Thou canst not will their endless death;
    Cast not their souls away.

O prosper these my earnest prayers,
Accept my never ceasing cares
    To bring them up for thee;
The help thou only canst afford,
Let nothing e'er provoke thee, Lord,
    To cease from granting me.

Assist me, with unwearied toil,
To clear and cultivate the soil,
    That all some crop may bear;
The stones to pluck, the thorns to burn,
The wayside path to dig and turn,
    And root out every tare.

Then be thy sun in strength revealed,
May dews of grace refresh my field,
    And gales reviving blow;
And when, obedient to thy word,
The heavenly seed I plant, O Lord,
    Make it take root and grow.

May each fond object of my love
Hereafter reign with thee above,
    And show forth here thy praise;
This boon of thee, Lord, I require,
For this my hope and chief desire,
    My voice I'll daily raise.

A prayer

Lord, who thy gifts hast freely showered,
And choicest blessings on me poured,
   Accept my grateful praise;
Thou canst supply my every want;
Thou hast engaged my prayer to grant,
   And keep me all my days.

Yet if thy wisdom see it right,
That with temptations I should fight
   To gain my heavenly crown,
Be thou at hand to cheer my way,
And give me patience day by day
   To choose thy will alone.

And grant that nothing thou hast given
May ever wean my heart from heaven,
   Or be my idol – God;
Ne'er may I so unthankful be
As to prefer thy works to thee,
   And thus require thy rod.

May pleasure, business, friends, retire,
Be God alone my heart's desire,
   My one chief needed bliss,
Of all things then I am secure,
For he hath said they shall be sure
   To all who're truly his.

Abraham's temptation

The setting sun had shed his parting ray,
Earth's colours faded one by one away,
The star of evening, firstborn of the sky,
Gazed mildly on the scene with bright'ning eye.
The cattle slept beside the sheltered hill,
The shepherd 'neath a tree lay hushed and still,
The horned moon essayed, with faintest light,
To stay the dark'ning shadows of the night,
The purpled air, for day's departure mourned

And into crystal dewdrops, weeping, turned;
When, the loved hour of prayer and musing spent,
The hoary Patriarch sought his silent tent
To court repose, – yet could not rest his head,
Till he approached his much loved Isaac's bed,
There, as he listened for his breathings soft,
He blessed the boy, – he blessed his Giver, oft;
Deep thrilling, tender joys beyond control,
As there he listened, filled that old man's soul; –
"Thou, God," he said, "hast heard my earnest prayer,
And blessed me with a son so good and fair!
Loved beyond utt'rance, o'er all else on earth,
This life has been my heaven since Isaac's birth!
My Lord! Jehovah! how my heart o'erflows,
With gratitude no other father knows!
Words only can I give, O had I more,
To show how fondly I thy grace adore!
O had I power beyond all doubt to prove,
My boundless thankfulness for all thy love,
That love which made the aged shout for joy,
And blessed the barren with this peerless boy!"
He said, – and turned him to his couch to weep
For joy; – yet soon forgot his tears in sleep.
For peaceful slumbers, gift from heaven above
Are shed by angels o'er the souls they love.
Soft was his sleep, as infants' slumbers calm,
The friend of God, nor felt, nor feared alarm.
Yet slept not long, for in the dead of night,
His chamber shone with more than mid-day light,
Wondering, he started from his couch in fear,
For a still voice low whispered in his ear,
And by his prophet-name called, – "Abraham!"
The man of God replied, "Lord, here I am!"
The voice rejoined, "Abraham thy prayers are heard
Thou wouldst be proved – I take thee at thy word,
Thou makest boast of gratitude to heaven,
A trial of that gratitude is given!
Take now thy son, the offspring of thy prayers,
Joy of thy life, crown of thy hoary hairs,
Arise and take him to Moriah's land,

There on the Mount, which I shall then command,
Slay him, – a sacrifice to God who gave,
And make the sacred flames his shroud and grave!"
He ceased – the Patriarch looked – the light was gone,
And *he,* left with his bleeding thoughts alone!
He turned to sleep – he said, "I did but dream!
That light was but the moonlight's parting beam!
But no! alas! it cannot, may not be!
The voice of God too well is known to me,
Oft have I heard it in the silent eve,
And well I loved to hearken and believe!
But then it was a messenger of good,
And now it bids me spill my first-born's blood,
My God! my God! Oh bid me die instead!"
Speaking, he sprang in anguish from his bed,
And sought a refuge in the midnight air,
From thoughts that breathed of madness and despair,
He raised in prayer his trembling hands on high,
He turned his aching eyes towards the sky;
Dark was the night, the moon's pale light all gone,
But countless stars, in southern splendour shone.
"Swore not the Lord," he cried, – "in truth and deed
That countless as those orbs should be my seed?
And said he not, that these should owe their life,
To Isaac – now to perish by my knife?
How can I doom to this untimely death,
The child who owes to me his form and breath?
How gladly could I save him, would I die!
O God accept a ransom! here am I!
It cannot be! the Lord no answer deigns,
No course but meek submission there remains;
The God who asks my son, he can restore,
I will believe, obey, nor murmur more.
I will invoke assistance from on high,
T'uphold me in this grievous agony!"
To him who smote, he prayed to heal his woes,
Then sought once more his swollen lids to close,
Long tears, now tears of agony, he wept,
At last worn nature yielded, and he slept.
Yet not in sleep was he from grief exempt,

The woes he waking felt, he sleeping dreamt.
But ere the dawn had chased the twilight grey,
Long ere the rising of the lamp of day,
The Patriarch rose, – with hasty step and wild,
He sought the chamber of his destined child,
Aroused him softly, with the gentlest care,
And bid him hasten and his journey share.
Himself, with pious hands prepared the wood,
The sacred fire, the necessary food,
Saddled his ass, – then with a scanty train,
Commenced his northward road across the plain.
For many a weary mile they urge their way,
How long to Abram, seemed each tedious day!
How did his boy's sweet converse wound his heart,
How at each sentence did his spirit smart,
How did his merry laugh, and joyous tongue,
Grieve the fond sire as on each word he hung!
Grieve! 'twere a mocking word to speak his pain,
Each was a stroke that clave his heart in twain!
But hours, however long, must end at last,
The first, and now the second eve is past,
Around he often turned his wearied sight,
And many a hill perceived, but none the right.
But at the dawning of the fatal day,
Behold Moriah's hill, though far away!
"'Tis the last time that to my treasure's eyes,
That glorious orb of day shall e'er arise!
'Tis the last time my darkening sight shall see,
All that earth holds, most loved and prized by me,
Ere yet that sun the eastern skies have left,
I shall be desolate, undone, bereft!
But shall these menials, with a curious eye,
On nature's grievous conflict coldly pry?
No! hold young men, I pray you tarry here,
My son and I design to worship near
Await below, an offering must I burn,
Then will I quickly to this spot return."
They mount the hill – with agile step, before,
Young Isaac trod, and his wood altar bore.
Behind, with lingering foot, the heart-rent sire,

Pressed to his doom, – and held the hallowed fire.
Silent they travelled long – the musing boy,
Sought, his pure mind in heavenly thoughts t'employ,
While his fond father pondered in his heart,
How best the fatal secret to impart.
Isaac at length the mournful silence broke,
As, starting from his musings, thus he spoke: -
"My father! if to sacrifice we came,
Here is the wood, the fire, but where the lamb?"
"My son," the Patriarch said, "Whate'er betide,
Trust thou in God, he will a lamb provide."
Again in silence they ascend the hill.
All nature, as in sympathy, is still,
The mountain bird suspends her early song,
The streamlet murmurs silently along,
The beast of prey forgets his savage growl,
The wolves shrink back and cease their fearful howl.
At length they reach, alas! the appointed spot,
The lamb, young Isaac seeks, but finds it not.
His father piles the wood in order meet,
There with his treasured boy he takes his seat,
He clasps his much-loved form in fond embrace,
Then lowly supplicates the throne of grace
For heavenly might, and courage to control,
The fearful thoughts that agitate his soul.
Then seeks for fitting phrases, to unfold,
The dreadful fate he may no more withhold.
"My son," he said, "ere on this sacred day,
Our bidden offerings to the Lord we pay,
I would thou mightest somewhat understand;
The rites we follow by our God's command.
These bloody offerings, my son, foreshow
Some promised gift, yet what I scarcely know;
To some great era time is hasting on,
When fallen man shall to God's grace be won,
When heaven shall purge the fault of our first sire,
And Adam's race escape their Maker's ire.
Further l oft have asked, but God's reply,
Forbids me in his mysteries to pry.
Yet hath he promised, ere to death I go,

More of these hidden wonders I shall know;
I wait his time, and now by strict command,
I come to worship in this distant land;
Thee have I brought, my firstborn, and my heir,
To cheer my journey, and assist my prayer,
Oft have I heard thee grateful anthems raise,
Oft hast thou joined with me in prayer and praise,
Then say my child dost thou my Maker love?"
"My father, yes, all earthly things above!"
"But did he need a proof, what wouldst thou give?"
"Father, thou knowest I but to serve him live!
Then let him ask of me whate'er he will,
My pleasure is, his pleasure to fulfil,
E'en should he ask the life he doth bestow,
My heart's blood freely in his cause should flow!"
"My son! thy lips have said the fearful word!
Thou art the lamb selected by our Lord!
Thy blood on this high mount he bids me spill!"
"Then haste, O father! the command fulfil!
You cannot hesitate to do his will.
See, I am ready, to my breast I bare!
Be thou resigned, I die without a care.
Yet Oh! my mother! would that she were here!
But for her sake I had not shed a tear.
Tell her, my only pang on leaving earth,
Was for *their* grief to whom I owe my birth.
And now dear father, wherefore this delay?
Bind me, complete the sacrifice, I pray;
Think not of me with pity, fear, or woe,
Who shall thus soon heaven's sweet enjoyments know,
Yes think of me, but with soft pleasure think,
I go the streams of Paradise to drink;
Soon the sweet food of Angels shall I eat,
How soon shall worship at my Maker's feet!
Detain me not my sire, I pray thee, not!
Fair is my hope, and truly blessed my lot;
My bounding soul pants for her hoped-for rest,
My spirit longs to join the righteous blessed!"
The Patriarch then, with courage of despair,
Binds with rude cords those members soft and fair,

Those feet that ever flew to do his will.
Hands, wont his smallest wishes to fulfil!
Sad task! but all submissively 'tis done,
And on the wood is laid his only son.
Unshrinkingly the Prophet lifts his knife,
One instant more had closed the victim's life!
When sudden light invests the lowering skies;
He stays his hand, and starting, lifts his eyes,
Once more the Lord addressed him from on high, –
"Abraham!" again he answered "here am I!"
"Hold!" said the voice, "and hear thou my command,
Nor on thy virtuous offspring, lay thy hand!
Enough thou hast been tried, now well I see,
That nought on earth thou dost prefer to me.
Now know I, that not e'en parental love,
Hath power thy tried fidelity to move,
Or shake thy well-placed fear reposed above!"
The grateful father, sinking on his knees,
Pours forth his thanks, then his loved boy he frees,
One moment gazes on his glowing face,
Then locks him in a breathless long embrace!
Nature's first transport scarcely yet was o'er,
They lift their eyes in joyous praise once more
When in a neighbouring thicket they behold,
An ancient ram, strayed from some distant fold;
His bushy horns were in a thicket caught,
Him quickly freed, and to the altar brought;
The Prophet slew with prayers, and vows of joy,
Vicarious offering for his rescued boy.
His sacrifice complete, once more the Lord
Spake to his faithful friend this parting word,
"Because, O Abraham! thou this deed hast done,
Nor spared from me thy son, thine only son,
Now by mine own all hallowed name I swear,
That thou shalt evermore my favour share,
In blessing, thee will I remember first,
Be all that love thee blessed! thy foes accursed!
An offspring numerous shall to thee be given,
As those bright stars that nightly shine in heaven,
Yea count the sands that gird the ocean's shore,

So many shall thy children be, and more,
I will afflict and wound their enemies,
While they shall be exalted to the skies!
And more, – through one to count from thee his birth,
Be blessed and saved all nations of the earth;
In this thy seed shall all mankind rejoice,
Because, when tried, thou hast obeyed my voice!"
Thus said the Lord, and to his servant's heart,
New stores of heavenly wisdom did impart;
Abram could now the veil of time withdraw,
Now in his boy, Messiah's type he saw;
He saw and knew, that on some distant day,
God's Son should on that hill man's ransom pay,
He saw him from his bed of death arise,
He saw him mount again his native skies,
He saw his offspring by a wondrous birth,
Spring in a day, and fill the joyous earth!
He saw, – and resting on his Maker's word,
His soul rejoiced, believing on the Lord

"All live unto him"

"I am" saith Christ "the life."
    Life of my soul thou art!
Thy words, 'mid sorrow, pain and strife,
    Bring comfort to my heart.

Thou art my life; – *by* thee
    Those live who love thy name;
From endless death with joy I flee,
    And thy free grace proclaim.

To thee O Lord I live,
    For my sake, who hast died;
For my life thou thine own didst give,
    And much endured beside.

With thee I live; for though
    Thou 'rt now exalted high,
Thy heart is with thy church below,
    Who for thy presence sigh.

Blest thought! that ever near
    Is he whom I adore;
I see by faith his glories here,
    And daily love him more.

But when I join, above,
    The assembly of the blest,
In worthier strains I'll praise his love
    In heaven's eternal rest.

And this, by grace, I'll do
    While here below I stay,
To Christ, *by* him and *with* him too,
    I'll live by night and day.

An evening hymn

Another day of peace and grace
    Now hastens to its close.
I seek once more, O Lord, thy face,
    Then yield me to repose:
        How blest are they,
        Who night and day,
In childlike confidence can pray!

I thank thee that this day was spent,
    In walking on toward heaven;
Lord, have I sinned? I do repent!
    O may I be forgiven!
        My prayer I make
        For Jesu's sake
That I his Spirit may partake.

Has health been mine? I thank thee, Lord,
    For this and every gift.
To thee, for all thou dost afford,
    My heart in praise I lift:
        That heart retain!
        For ne'er again
Would I be led by trifles vain.

I am, my much loved Saviour, thine;
   O let me to thee live;
Free love is all that can be mine;
    That little all I give!
       O let me still
       Thy laws fulfil,
No choice have I, no other will!

O be with me kind Lord this night,
   While my tired senses sleep;
It is thine office, thy delight,
    Those who trust thee to keep.
       The low, and meek,
       Thy ways who seek,
These dost thou love, though faint and weak.

Lord, deign to keep my every friend
   Though far they live from me,
Health, pardon, peace, redemption send,
    From evil may they flee;
       O may we each,
       Those mansions reach,
Whose road, thyself hast died to teach!

An evening hymn

Lord, I close my eyes to sleep,
Knowing thou wilt vigils keep;
Tranquilly I sink to rest,
All my daily sins confessed;
     O speak the word,
      Forgive them, Lord!
And to my trembling soul thy peace afford!

Let me think upon the day
Thou shalt call my soul away;
When I lay me down to die,
Be thou to uphold me nigh.
     O calm my fears,
      And dry my tears,
As now thy grace my fearful spirit cheers.

Lord! preserve me through the night,
Joyfully I'll hail the light;
Thou to death shall be my guide
And my trust whate'er betide;
    And when mine eyes
    In Paradise
Shall see thee first, how joyful my surprise!

An evening hymn

Lord, I now retire to rest,
May my soul by thee be blest.
Let me, Lord, thy favour share,
Make me thy peculiar care,
So that safe from harm and foes,
Tranquilly I may repose.

In the morning when I wake
Let me still thy care partake;
May I well the day begin,
Keep me till its close from sin;
Sin above all else I fear,
Ne'er may I its witcheries hear.

Keep this night each cherished friend,
On them choicest blessings send;
May they fix their hearts on thee,
May they all temptation flee;
For I hope to meet above
All whom here below I love!

An evening prayer

Once more I arrive at the close of the day,
Be thou my Protector my Father, I pray.
For Jesus' dear sake spread thy wings o'er my head,
And guard me from sickness, from harm and from dread.

From all wicked thoughts my arch foe would suggest,
To deaden my conscience, and sully my breast;
From all bad desires of my own perverse mind,
Protect me O thou, my preserver and friend!

O may my first thoughts, when tomorrow I wake,
Be of him who endured all death's pains for my sake;
And grant that my life from henceforward may prove,
My grateful obedience, my faith and my love!

An evening prayer

Saviour! my evening prayers receive,
    Accept my sacrifice of praise;
Remit the sins for which I grieve,
    The sins of this and former days.

O give me future strength, my God,
    To choose the good and flee the ill;
Make me resigned beneath thy rod,
    Submissive to thy holy will.

That heavenly purity impart,
    Without which none can see thy face;
Give me a free and upright heart,
    Cleansed and made perfect by thy grace!

O make me thankful for the care,
    The love that crowns with gifts my life,
That bids me all earth's comforts share,
    And shields me from its woes and strife.

Protect this night from every harm,
    Myself, and all who share my love;
Pour in our souls celestial balm,
    And raise us earth's delights above!

"And be thankful"

Thankful! thankful! yes I am
For thy death, thou holy Lamb!
Thankful may I ever be
For thy wondrous love to me.

Sayest thou, "Remember me!"?
I remember joyfully;
Ever while my life shall last
Will I hold thy memory fast.

May thy body, gracious Lord,
Endless life to mine afford;
May it vivify my soul,
Feed, refresh, and make it whole.

May I, when I take and eat,
Humbly kneeling at thy feet,
Feed on Jesus as he saith,
Thankfully in humble faith.

When the holy cup I drink
On his bitter woes I'll think,
How his precious blood was shed,
How, for me, it was he bled.

Surely Lord I'll think on thee!
But wilt thou remember me?
High exalted as thou art,
Carest thou to claim my heart?

When the beggar at the gate,
For an alms implores the great,
Is he of assistance sure?
Is his claim that he is poor?

When the wretch, of all bereft,
Says "I desolate am left",
Do his friends rejoice the more,
To receive him than before?

Will the bitterest regret
Pay the ruined merchant's debt?
Would the felon grace receive
If he for his crimes should grieve?

Courtiers draw not near the throne,
But with princely garments on;
If in sordid rags they came,
Would they not be put to shame?

How then can I hope, O Lord,
To be welcome at thy board?
No fit garments can I boast,
I my courtly robes have lost.

Riches! – none do I possess,
No one ever boasted less;
I am deeply in thy debt,
Canst thou all I owe forget?

Can I venture to approach
Free from blame, without reproach?
Shall I dare address my King?
Gifts! – I have not one to bring!

Yes, the voice of Jesus cries,
"Come poor sinner, haste, arise,
Thou hast not wherewith to buy,
But I will thy wants supply;

Fitting garment hast thou none?
Hearken, I have wrought thee one;
Thou art black, but seek the flood,
Wash thee in my cleansing blood;

Riches, suppliant dost thou want?
Boundless wealth I to thee grant,
And thy debts, they all were paid,
Ere I in the tomb was laid;

Honours, favours, dost thou need?
These thy portion are decreed;
Dost thou seek to wear a crown?
Wait and thou shalt share my own;

Seek'st thou more poor sinner, say?"
"Lord", I boldly answer, – "yea,
Make me sure, I own thy love,
This I prize all gifts above.

Should'st thou give me all the earth,
More than that thy love is worth,
Thou so much hast promised me,
Yet content I cannot be;

Satisfied I shall not rest,
Till with thine affection blessed,
All for this I'd freely give,
And content, though poor, could live.

Grant me Saviour my request,
Come and make my heart thy rest,
Come and make thy promise good,
Be my life, my light, my food."

"As thy day so shall thy strength be"

O God thou hast, unasked,
    To us a promise made,
That in our woes thy aid should last,
    As long as man should need,
And that whate'er our *day* might be,
There should be needful strength from thee.

My life, Lord, is that day,
   'Tis often clouded o'er,
And then, how oft I lose my way,
   And need thy help implore,
That I may not my road forsake,
Nor smoother paths of pleasure take.

Often my thoughts are sad
   When looking back on life,
To see so much that's really bad,
   So little earnest strife
Against myself, the world and sin,
My foes both outward and within.

But when I shall look back
   On what is yet to come.
O may the view no more be black
   With duties left undone,
With errors both by deed and word,
Repentance slighted or deferred.

But not in mine own strength,
   'Tis not myself I trust,
For humbled by my falls, at length,
   I lowly kiss the dust,
And look to God's assisting arm,
To guard my soul from future harm.

And he will not, I know,
   My humble call despise;
He grieves when sin has brought us low,
   And urges us to rise;
Who ever tried him in distress?
Let *him* declare God's faithfulness!

Birthday thoughts

Again the fleeting year is past,
    My birthday comes again;
Each year seems shorter than the last,
The seasons fly away more fast,
    Life's joys seem all more vain.

'Tis not without a secret sigh,
    I think upon this day,
How often has my heart beat high,
To see its dawn in years gone by,
    Years ever past away.

Though always by my friends caressed
    In childhood's years of bliss,
This day they seemed to love me best,
And favour me o'er all the rest;
    A happy day was this!

Yet let me not the past forget,
    Nor sigh for pleasures fled;
'Tis sinful and unwise to fret,
And many blessings are there yet
    Showered daily on my head.

Though parted from my early friends,
    Sweet hopes my spirits cheer,
That in the life which never ends,
Union unchecked shall make amends
    For pain of absence here.

Nor do I quite the hope resign
    That even on this earth,
It may be yet thy will divine
T' unite me to those friends of mine
    Who've loved me from my birth.

These are my fairest dreams of bliss;
    And if it be God's will,
(For I desire to bend to his,)
Perhaps he may accord me this,
    And all my hopes fulfil.

And O! may the ensuing year
    Be prosperous to us all;
Lord, banish every cause of fear,
Our spirits sanctify and cheer
    Whatever us befall.

If death our family invade,
    And break our circle up,
When in the earth our friends are laid,
Though broken-hearted, not dismayed,
    Resigned we'll drink the cup.

Bright hopes of future bliss shall cheer
    The sorrow-stricken heart;
If thus bereft we find life drear;
No matter! grief brings heaven more near,
    And warns us to depart.

For this low earth is not our rest,
    Nor human love our all,
In heaven we shall be truly blest,
And Jesus' love is far the best,
    Sure, – whatsoe'er befall.

Claims of the heathen

O Lord of Hosts! to me impart
    A portion of thy zeal;
And make this thoughtless, selfish heart
    For others' sorrows feel.

Enlarge it Lord, that it may hold
    All who may need relief,
All, to sin's iron bondage sold,
    All who are bent with grief.

For, ah! our brethren near us live
    In misery and woe;
And if the smallest alms we give,
    We boast what good we do!

The young, the ignorant, the old,
    Instruction loudly ask;
But we can yet our aid withhold
    Because 'tis others' task!

The heathen groan in Satan's chains,
    No paths of peace they know,
Perhaps foredoomed to endless pains!
    And we would have it so.

"A God of grace is ours," we say,
    "And never will decree,
The heathen to be cast away,
    That, Lord, be far from thee."

And so we go not to their aid,
    Our pity we withhold,
Our prayers are languid and delayed,
    We scarce will spare our gold.

But at the coming judgment-day,
    When we together stand,
What will these now despised ones say,
    Who'll flock from every land?

"Lord we were hungry, and these gave
    No manna for our soul,
Oppressed, and none arose to save
    From sin's all-powerful rule.

"We thirsted for the Spirit's grace,
    No living waters came;
Unclothed with Jesus' righteousness,
    They left us in our shame.

"Sick and imprisoned was our soul,
    They visited us not;
The healing leaves had made them whole,
    Our wounds were all forgot."

How shall we answer in that day,
    To such a charge as this?
Think we, if they are cast away,
    Ourselves can hope for bliss?

No! for the Judge in thunder's tone,
    Shall thus rehearse our doom,
"Depart ye heartless ones! begone,
    To hell's accursed tomb!"

God grant, a lot so desolate,
    May never fall to me,
But now, e'er death shall seal my fate,
    My duty may I see!

Grant me my neighbour's good to seek,
    For soul and body too,
Grant me the words of faith to speak,
    The work of grace to do!

And when the judgment hour shall come,
    May Jesus say to me,
"O welcome to the eternal home
    Prepared of old for thee!"

Compassion for the heathen

Children of the Living God!
Ye who in his ways have trod,
Ye who in confiding faith
Trust whate'er your Father saith;
Ye of Jesus' love possessed,
Heirs of Heaven's eternal rest,
Weep for them who never knew
All the hopes so dear to you!

Weep for those, who, lost to shame,
Boastingly their guilt proclaim;
Worshippers of wood and stone,
Who 'neath Satan's terrors groan;
Men who shed their parents' blood,
Drown their babes in Gunga's flood;
Weep for them! they never knew
Him who died for them and you!

Weep for them! but while ye weep,
Strive to break their death-like sleep;
They are hurrying to the grave,
Hasten! strive their souls to save!
Think not toil and prayer are vain,
Prayer and toil their souls might gain!
Try! – for Christ whom ne'er they knew,
Died for them as well as you.

Confession

O Lord my God, thou God of grace!
In lowly grief I seek thy face;
O deign my fears and doubts to chase
    While in thy courts I bow;
Thus oft, and oft in days of yore,
My errors here did I deplore,
Then rose and sinned just as before:
    My guilt is great, I know!

But may it ne'er be thus again!
O let not all remorse's pain,
Let not my vows and prayers be vain
    More grace to me afford!
For long, O Lord, alas! how long,
I've wandered sinful joys among,
Though good I knew, I yet did wrong;
    And sinned by thought and word!

But O! once more renew my soul,
Forgive the past and make me whole,
And all my future life control,
    O thou my hope alone!
Take Satan's power to harm, away,
In earnest faith thine aid I pray;
When tempted, give me grace to say,
    "Foul spirit, hence, be gone!"

O take away the love of ill,
Say to my roving thoughts, "be still!"
And my vain heart with wisdom fill
    That I may sin no more:
For though the evil fiends depart,
Great is their fraud and subtle art,
And they will seek to make my heart
    Their dwelling, as before.

And though they find it cleansed and swept,
With all its former vileness wept,
And new resolves with strictness kept,
    Such is their guile and skill, –
That if no rival guest it hold,
They enter in with daring bold,
And take their station as of old,
    More strong to work it ill.

Then lest they ever should again
An entrance to my heart obtain
And make thy grace and pardon vain,
    Now, ere it be too late,
I'll seek a better, stronger guest,
And pray he'll come and take his rest,
And make his home within my breast,
    And then I'll close its gate: –

Nor yet shall all my care be o'er,
Watchings and prayers shall guard the door
Lest sleepless sin creep in once more
   And chase my heavenly guest.
And I will pray thee, Lord of light!
To aid me in this weary fight,
And speed the cause of truth and right
   As it shall seem thee best.

Yes, Lord, I firmly trust in thee!
E'en now by faith the day I see
When Satan's power no more shall be,
   Thy saints to harm and grieve;
Thine hour of vengeance comes at last,
To lowest hell he bound is cast,
And all his bloated power is past
   The nations to deceive!

Consolation in distress

Fret not thyself, O child of woe,
   Though troubles may be thine;
Thy Saviour ruleth all below,
   How canst thou then repine!

These trials which thy courage shake,
   And all thy patience try,
Are sent the bonds of sin to break,
   And fix thy hopes on high.

Are they too many or too great?
   Before thou judge they are,
Think of thy sins and all their weight;
   Can they with them compare?

Most true it is that all earth's pains
   Could not for sin atone,
One only hope for man remains,
   'Tis in what Christ hath done.

Yet sufferings are appointed means,
    By which from sin and earth,
Jesus his children often weans,
    And teaches them his worth.

In all my sorrows then may I
    By his, fresh courage take;
And when my sins against me cry,
    His cross my refuge make.

Consolatory thoughts

When anxious cares disturb my soul,
And grief's dark clouds above me roll;
When by foreboding fears oppressed,
In vain I seek for peace or rest;
How sweet to know I have a friend,
Whose love and pity have no end.

When lying on the bed of pain.
And praying for relief in vain,
When forced to practise self-denial,
Or crossed by many a vexing trial;
O then I prize heaven's peaceful rest,
And own that to depart is best.

When conscience' startling voice within
Alarms the soul for all its sin;
When memory sleeping now no more,
Recounts past sins forgot before;
O then thrice happy, if I know
The refuge from this maddening woe!

But when life's parting hour draws nigh,
And in the arms of death I lie
When to a land, now quite unknown,
My trembling, wandering soul has flown,
Who shall my refuge be but thou?
No other refuge have I now.

Whom have I Lord in heaven but thee,
And whom on earth so dear to me?
No friends who my affection share,
So loving or so constant are,
How happy is the Christian's case,
To share so kind a Master's grace.

O Jesus! man's unchanging friend;
To me thy favours still extend!
In death and life, in weal and woe,
Thy wonted kindness ever show;
And in return thy name I'll praise,
And dedicate to thee my days !

"Deliver us from evil"

How sadly inconstant am I!
    I purpose each morning anew,
From every temptation to fly,
    And heaven and virtue pursue.

But yet when the tempter essays,
    To win back my heart unto sin,
My passions are all in a blaze,
    And mock the resistance within.

Now heavenward I'm ready to fly;
    Now sinfully clinging to earth,
This hour to all sin I would die,
    The next 'tis my solace and mirth.

Great God! fix my wandering heart,
    I pray thee, for Jesus' sake,
Thy saving correction impart
    My soul from her sleep to awake.

For I cannot do it, good Lord,
    Thou knowest I have often essayed,
Thou only canst succour afford,
    O let not thy help be delayed:

For short as a span are my days,
  Be swift then to rescue my soul;
And thine be the glory and praise,
  When I, by thy grace, am made whole.

Duty of prayer for missionaries

Shall the heralds who proclaim,
To lost men a Saviour's name,
They who country leave, and home,
And to savage regions roam,
Be forgotten in your prayer?
Shall they no kind wishes share?

Did not Jesus say to all,
"To my church the heathen call;
To earth's utmost verges go,
Let each soul my gospel know"?
These, their Lord's commands obey –
Surely ye will for them pray!

Lost would all mankind have been,
Had not God their misery seen,
And with merciful ones intent
His beloved, to save them, sent;
Ye who missionaries contemn,
Think on Christ at Bethlehem!

Tell me, ye who scorn and doubt them,
What had Britain been without them?
Till the light and power of grace,
Came, her night of sin to chase,
Lost in ignorance and woe,
What but evil did she know?

Ye then who in Britain dwell, –
Ye whom Christ redeemed from hell,
God's rich benefits repay,
With what poor returns ye may!
Do your utmost, give your all,
The return would still be small.

To the heathen can *you* go?
"Surely," you will answer, "No!"
Others offer in your stead,
All they ask is daily bread;
That, your prayers, and sympathy,
Can you in their need deny?

'Tis the least that you can do,
While they strive and toil for you;
Leave them not to break their hearts;
In their labours take your parts.
So, when God their work shall crown,
Their reward shall be your own.

"Fear not little flock"

Fear not, little flock! said the Saviour we love,
For yours is the kingdom that comes from above,
Fear not little flock for to you shall be given,
('Tis my Father's good pleasure) the kingdom of heaven.

Small then was thy flock, blessed Shepherd, to keep.
And soon wast thou smitten and scattered thy sheep,
Yet there in thy word stood this promise the same,
My kingdom shall come, earth shall hallow my name.

Not long didst thou make earth's cold chambers thy bed;
Thy rising, to us, was as life to the dead;
Rejoiced by thy presence, thy heralds went forth,
And spread thy glad message from south unto north.

Thy sheep heard the call, and came forth at thy word,
And gladly they suffered, or died for their Lord;
They said to their foes, "You are sending us home
To rest till our Lord to his kingdom shall come."

The years swiftly passed, and the church changed her foes,
The beast from the sea, in his terrors arose;
A wolf in sheep's clothing was he, and awhile,
Full well he succeeded the sheep to beguile.

He grasped the young lambs in his pitiless hold,
He turned out the shepherds, and ruled in the fold;
He poisoned the streams, and the pastures he trod,
He told the poor flock, 'twas the will of their God.

Then glad were the sheep to escape from the fold,
A refuge to seek in the mountain's strong hold;
And in their distress they consoled themselves thus,
"Our Master has promised his kingdom to us."

The day of their trials and griefs at length passed,
Their foes in their turn were afflicted at last,
And the sheep surely slept as their Shepherd had said,
And ate their own pastures, none made them afraid.

Now quietly feed they, from terrors secure,
Their fold is enlarged, and their waters are sure;
They lift up their heads as the promise draws nigh,
And look for the city that comes from the sky!

Their king too will come! – now why waitest thou Lord?
O come and accomplish thine own gracious word!
The flock which thou leftest so faint and so small,
Look now, and a numberless host thou shalt call.

O why dost thou linger? the time, sure, is come,
Thy children are waiting to welcome thee home;
Long, long have they reckoned the years and the days,
And mourned that their Saviour his coming delays.

His time is *not* come! – till his angels collect
From the four winds of heaven his scattered elect;
His time is not come till the Jews be restored,
Till earth's farthest borders shall own him as Lord.

He comes not till then! yet if so who would sleep?
Arouse ye, O shepherds, and seek for your sheep!
Search all the world round, call aloud in his name,
Your Master's kind message to all men proclaim.

O urge them, intreat them, compel them to come!
Point out the safe fold, bid them make it their home;
And tell them their Lord now his coming delays,
That they may have space to consider their ways.

"Feed my sheep"

If now the Lord, as once of old,
    Enquired, "Say, lov'st thou me?"
And I replied with answer bold,
    "Thou knowest I love thee!"
Would not his words my conscience move?
"Feed then my sheep thy boast to prove."

Are these his words? and have I slept,
    Neglecting them so long?
I knew they were, – yet never kept
    One lamb from going wrong;
But still how patiently he bears,
And me, his careless shepherd spares!

Even the hireling, only flies,
    When danger is at hand;
But I in days of peace despise
    My Saviour's last command;
How can he in his service keep,
One who dares thus neglect his sheep?

Lord! now at last thy lambs I'll feed
    If thou still grant me grace;
And, while I seek the aid I need
    Each day before thy face,
Dear Saviour! my endeavours crown,
And make my children all thine own!

For a passionate person

Can I a disciple be,
Meek and gentle Lord, of thee?
How should then ungoverned wrath,
Ever from my lips burst forth?

Can I be thy servant, Lord,
And sin thus by deed and word?
Can I thus with passion shake,
And thy precepts fail to break?

On my foes I vengeance wreak,
Christ says "blessed are the meek,"
I my enemies detest,
Christ, the merciful, hath blessed.

Though my spirit scorns t'endure,
He says "blessed are the poor,"
Think I in revenge to live?
Jesus saith "thou shalt forgive."

Lord! humility impart
To my proud relentless heart;
Never may the flesh obtain
Such a victory again.

Lord, thy pardon I request;
I have all my sin confessed.
Wash me from this grievous stain!
Wash me! or my tears are vain.

Thou, who didst thy foes forgive,
Bid thy sorrowing suppliant live.
Let me by thy pattern learn
Good for evil to return.

Then, with more of truth, I may
That I'm thy disciple say;
Grant me thus, though weak and frail,
O'er my passions to prevail.

For a time of pestilence

Death I know is ever near.
    But, nearer now than ever,
May its salutary fear
Make our hopes of heaven more dear,
    And from this earth us sever.

Who, but those to Christ who flee,
    And hope for his salvation,
Can resigned and cheerful be
When black pestilence they see
    Thus desolate our nation?

Some may fortify their mind,
    Or trust their constitution;
Some be to their danger blind,
Safety hope by flight to find,
    Or steadfast resolution:

But the Christian calm can stand,
    Surrounded thus by sorrow;
Well he knows by whose command
Sickness desolates a land,
    And fears not for the morrow.

Death may call his friends away, –
    That will but make Christ dearer;
Pestilence himself may slay
Ere is past another day, –
    He hails what brings heaven nearer.

If God's pleasure it should be,
    He yields with meek submission;
He, to him who smites, can flee,
Bend to his all just decree,
    And for his grace petition.

Be this, Lord, our favoured case;
    And then, whate'er befall us,
We all anxious thoughts may chase,
Knowing heaven's our dwelling place
    Whene'er thou hence shall call us.

For Saturday night

Another week alas! is gone –
    O time too quickly fled!
And all is silence, and alone
    I rest my weary head.

Six days in industry and care
    By thy command I spend.
This makes the Sabbath doubly fair
    When all my labours end.

To fit me for its duties, Lord,
    I'll rise betimes and pray;
I'll read and ponder on thy word,
    That lamp which guides my way.

When in thy courts, a blessing give
    On all I read and hear.
O give thy servant grace to live,
    For ever in thy fear.

All sins committed this last week
    Blot out, Lord, and remit;
And for the future, grace I seek
    All sinful ways to quit.

Give us, day by day our daily bread

O it is good, 'tis sweet to me,
Thy pensioner, dear Lord, to be;
And every day and hour to live
On what thy charity may give.

Of worldly things I ask no store,
Food when 'tis needed, not before;
A shelter from bleak winter's cold,
And rest from toil when I am old.

At night a pillow for my head,
"In sickness, thee to make my bed,"
A refuge in affliction's blast,
And hopes of bliss when life is past.

These things, as needed, thou shalt give,
Thy daily pensioner I live.
Not for a year's supply today;
For grace in time of need I pray.

'Tis well Lord that it thus should be;
It draws the soul more near to thee.
And thus we two-fold blessings share,
Blessed is thy answer, blessed our prayer.

Happiness

Sweet Happiness! thy presence show;
Without thee earth is nought but woe,
    O say, where art thou found?
Dost thou in busy cities dwell?
Or in the lonely, peaceful dell?
    Or, but in fairy ground?

Thee, men have sought through all the earth,
In gold, in honours, pomp, and mirth,
   And but thy shadow gain;
Is there no spot but has been trod
In seeking for thy blest abode?
   Is all our search in vain?

"Blind mortal!" Happiness replies,
"My dwelling is beyond the skies,
   'Tis vain to search below;
And he whose hopes are centred here,
Although he oft may think me near,
   Shall ne'er my sweetness know.

But turn thy heart to things above,
Thy God and Saviour fear and love,
   And fly from every sin;
So thou shalt taste e'en here below,
Such joys as Christians only know,
   Which heaven on earth begin.

Thy heart let God's high will employ.
Expect not here unmingled joy,
   But let God's will be thine;
The more thou patiently endure
Thou shalt hereafter (be thou sure),
   In heaven more brightly shine.

Then seek me not, my son, below,
But rather seek God's will to know,
   And daily grow in grace;
Strive all his pleasure to fulfil;
E'en angels have no other will
   Who see his glorious face.

In duty's path it is alone
That true and lasting joys are strewn,
   Descending from above;
And soon shall grace to thee be given,
This changing world to quit for heaven,
   Where all is peace and love."

Heaven

O what is heaven? it is the place
    Where sin no more hath sway,
Where basking in the Spirit's grace,
    'Tis nature to obey.

Earth's sunniest scenes, though bright and fair,
    Are clouded o'er by sin;
And 'mid sweet nature's gifts most rare
    Man's heart is dark within.

Some speak of heaven, – a land of flowers,
    Of music and of light,
Of shaded avenues, deep bowers,
    And sparkling streams and bright;

Of spotless robes, and amaranth crowns,
    And wings more swift than wind,
A land, where winter never frowns,
    Nor sorrow weighs the mind.

Sweet is the clime! yet 'tis not this,
    That makes it dear to me;
It is the thought, enchanting bliss!
    From sin we there are free.

There never more shall I offend
    The God whose smile is life;
There, never more in anguish bend
    To mourn sin's weary strife.

Here, oft when earth's fair scenes I see,
    My heart is dark within,
And heaven is chiefly heaven to me
    Because 'tis free from sin.

Hymn before the Lord's Supper

O Jesus, take my sins away,
    Before I at thy altar kneel!
Blessed Spirit, help thou me to pray,
    And help thou me sin's weight to feel!

O let me not approach, unmeet
    To share the grace thou dost dispense;
And be thou with me, I entreat,
    And wash my heart in innocence.

So let me to thine altar go,
    Repenting truly of my sin,
And firmly set thy will to do,
    And a new life of faith begin.

A lively faith do thou afford
    In God's kind mercies given through thee;
And make me thankful, dearest Lord,
    For all thou hast endured for me.

In love sincere to all mankind
    Would I approach thy house today.
And may I there the blessing find
    For which at home in vain I pray.

O grant thy presence, I entreat,
    While at thine altar I shall kneel;
O make me for thy service meet;
    My griefs, my sins, my errors heal.

Hymns for Sunday 1

Fairest day of all the seven,
Day of rest and type of heaven,
Morn that saw the Lord arise.
Welcome to my waking eyes!

All my weekly tasks are o'er,
Earthly cares intrude no more;
All that wearied and oppressed,
Now is past, and I may rest.

To the house of God I'll go,
Bending at his footstool low,
Every blessing to intreat,
At my heavenly Father's feet.

There I hear his gracious word,
There I thank and praise my Lord,
There my fainting powers renew
Every virtue to pursue.

Then my Saviour, be thou near;
Keep me in thy love and fear,
And may earth's sweet Sabbaths, blessed,
Fit me for eternal rest!

Hymns for Sunday 2

O may thy hallowed Sabbaths, Lord,
Such pleasure to our hearts afford
That we may not their joys forego
For ought this world has to bestow.

If sinners should our choice contemn,
More cause have we to pity them,
Whose sinful joys no comforts give
Like theirs who in God's service live.

'Tis not alone for duty's sake,
That we thy Sabbaths holy make;
It is our privilege and bliss
To keep God's day as only his.

All labour on this day we quit,
Our worldly pleasures we remit;
The Sabbath is our great delight,
And ever precious in our sight.

Thy Sabbaths Lord, as links of gold,
Draw those to heaven who firmly hold;
Each Sabbath day, more nigh we soar
To where the Sabbath ends no more.

Hymns for Sunday 3

This day, O Lord, is thine alone,
    One day in seven is thine;
To give unto thee, Lord, thine own,
    I will my heart incline.

All days to thee belong alone,
    But six to us are given,
On them thou bid'st us work, – on one,
    The seventh, prepare for heaven.

How truly merciful, how wise,
    Was this thy first command
Which unto all sweet rest supplies,
    Throughout each Christian land!

But when thy glorious kingdom shall
    Throughout the world extend;
And when the Christian nations all
    Their evil ways amend;

Then shall thy Sabbaths through the world,
    Be better far obeyed,
And Satan from his throne be hurled,
    While guilt sinks down in shade,

Then each shall seek his neighbour's good,
    Then each for all will care;
Earth gladly sing with wine and food,
    And joy and peace dwell there.

O could I live to see those days,
    How would my soul rejoice,
To hear glad strains of heartfelt praise
    Resound from every voice.

But O be mine the portion, Lord,
    Of saints in ancient story,
That I may trust thy promised word,
    And see by faith thy glory!

Hymns for Sunday 4

All hail! sweet Sabbath day!
    Day ever dear to me!
I cast all worldly cares away,
    And turn me, Lord, to thee;
One day of thine is better far
Than years of worldly pleasures are.

I know, at break of day
    On this most holy morn,
Thy servants often meet and pray,
    For Jesu's church forlorn;
I gladly join my voice to theirs,
And may success reward our prayers!

When to thy house I go,
    How sweet it is to think
That all my dearest friends below
    Of the same fountain drink;
At once thy gracious gifts intreat,
And sit at the same Saviour's feet.

Then if so sweet the rest
    Of Sabbaths here below,
How greatly, Lord, thy saints are blest
    Who endless Sabbaths know,
Who, every object of their love,
See near them, never to remove

But far more blest are they
    To see their Saviour's face,
To join in praising, night and day,
    The wonders of his grace;
Then show me, Lord, the nearest road,
Conduct me straight to their abode!

Hymns for Sunday 5

Day of rest from care and sadness,
    Be to me a rest indeed;
Be a day of peace and gladness,
    Safe from sin, from sorrow freed!

If my sins be left behind,
    Pardoned by God's tender love,
In his courts below I find
    Joy like that of saints above.

Lord of life! I come to purchase,
    Not with silver, nor with gold,
All the free eternal riches
    Which thy prophets have foretold.

Lord of life! reject not me,
    Father! hear thy contrite child,
Who desires from sin to flee,
    And to heaven be reconciled.

Guard, O guard my thoughtless soul,
    Lest from thee again I turn;
Let thy fear my heart control,
    Let thy love within me burn!

Hymns for Sunday 6

How great, Lord, thy mercy to man when thou sayest,
    "Six days for thy business are thine;
But 'tis my command that the seventh thou rest,
    For one day in seven is mine."

How sweet to the poor, the care-worn, the oppressed,
    To know that one day is their own,
How great the relief to the bosom distressed
    To approach in God's house, to his throne!

To pleasure's mad followers how good the restraints
    That check for a day their career;
But most it is precious, O Lord, to thy saints;
    To them it indeed is most dear.

How foolish, as well as how wicked, are they,
    Who despise all the good they might gain
By strictly devoting to Heaven this day; –
    What benefits thence they'd obtain.

How small, too, the pleasure they reap in return
    For indulging their sinful desire;
For remorse must their hearts, when in solitude, burn,
    And dread of unquenchable fire.

Aid *me* then, O Lord, preparation to make
    For worthily keeping the day;
All pleasures and worldly affairs I'll forsake,
    Earth's sorrows and cares, cast away.

"I am for peace"

Lord give me grace to bless
    All those who me offend;
Grant them their errors to confess,
    And causeless anger end.

Woe, woe, is me! to dwell
    Amidst the sons of strife.
O Christ, their warring spirits quell!
    They weary me of life.

I labour sore for peace;
    But when they see me yield,
Their bold exactions but increase,
    They arm them for the field.

When I resist their wrong,
    And seek to gain my due,
I'm their reproach and scornful song,
    They fiercely me pursue.

Then, lest with grief I faint,
    And yield me to despair,
To thee I make my humble plaint,
    O thou who hearest prayer!

Thou who didst once endure
    Reproach from sinful men,
Thou canst our evil tempers cure,
    And give us peace again.

O change my stubborn foes,
    Give them a fleshy heart.
Meanwhile, in pity to my woes,
    Patience divine impart.

For thou canst give me peace
    Though raging foes abound;
Yes, all my sorrows then shall cease
    When I thy peace have found.

"I am not alone"

Solitude is sweet to me,
Then I feel, Lord, nearer thee,
Then my spirit homeward flies
To thy dwelling in the skies.

Would I were, my God, with thee,
All thy excellence to see;
Would I could behold thy face,
Would I heard thy words of grace.

Very soon, I hope to soar
Where I shall desire no more;
Very soon to see my Lord,
Know his face, obey his word.

For on earth is not my rest,
I, a pilgrim am, confessed;
Here in tents I dwell content,
On my future home intent.

Frustrate not my hope I pray,
Haste and bear my soul away;
Thine abode is better far
Than all earth's enjoyments are.

"I am the way, the truth, and the life"

Who seeketh Heaven to reach?
　　Saith Christ, "I am the way,
And those that follow me shall each
　　Attain Heaven's endless day."

Who wisheth the truth to gain?
　　To Christ he must apply;
All needful wisdom they attain
　　Who ask it from on high.

Then would you 'scape from death?
　　He only life can give;
He gave at first our fleeting breath,
　　He bids our spirits live.

For all that thou hast given,
　　I pray to thee, my Lord;
Show me the way to Heaven;
　　Eternal life afford;
O be the guardian of my youth,
And ever lead me into truth!

"I say unto all – watch"

Help me, Lord, to understand
All that Scripture does command;
And when thine high will I know,
Grant me grace that will to do.

Help me meekly to receive
All a Christian should believe;
Day by day increase my faith
In whate'er the Bible saith.

Lord, thy prophecies unfold,
Till the future I behold,
And by faith thy glories view,
Ever bright and ever new!

Thou wilt come, as comes a thief,
Chase our sloth and unbelief;
May we hourly watch and pray,
And be waiting for thy day.

Lest the day of grace be lost
May thy watchers keep their post;
May they warn the heedless sheep
Safe within the fold to keep.

Let them seek the church to rouse
Ere the coming of her spouse,
See that she her lamp prepares,
And the wedding garment wears.

For her Lord is at the door;
He will warn her now no more
Till he comes, to seek his own;
And with them to share his throne.

Be prepared, ye sons of men,
For he comes, ye know not when;
But the time is surely near;
Will you not his coming fear?

He is coming as a king,
With him all his saints he'll bring;
Streaming fire before him flows
Breathing vengeance to his foes.

Turn, ye rebels, turn then now,
Humbly in his presence bow.
Seek him quickly for your friend,
Ere your day of grace shall end.

Ill spent time

Forgive me, O my God, I pray,
The hours I've misemployed today;
They ill thy scrutiny can stand,
Ill bear the test of thy command;
The hours of serious employ,
The time I love alone t'enjoy,
All used amiss! – what can I say?
Alas! for moments thrown away;
Tears and regrets are spent in vain,
What power can gather them again?
The man whose parting breath draws nigh,
With gold those hours would gladly buy,
And yet I've lavished them away,
Though this may e'en be *my* last day!
But what do grief and tears avail?
Can they to gain them back prevail?
No! that, nor earth nor heaven, could do.
In vain, in vain their loss I rue!
Nay, not in vain calm reason cries,
Not useless are those heartfelt sighs;
Though you can ne'er lost time regain,
Repentance is not useless pain;
First let it lead to Jesus' feet,
His pardon for the past t'intreat;
Then store its lessons in your mind
To arm you, when to ill inclined.
They oft must feel remorse's pain,
Who from the past no wisdom gain;
But they who mourn o'er every crime
Will conquer their defects in time,
Thus, though with strength and purpose frail,
I seek o'er evil to prevail;

But if my purpose I pursue
My fainting powers shall God renew;
From sins of thought, of word, of deed,
At last I shall by grace be freed.
Thus the refiner long will pore
Unwearied on his precious ore.
He heaps the fire when it decays,
Or damps, if it too fiercely blaze;
But when the ore his image shows
Its fitness for his use he knows.
And grief, like the refiner's fire,
God sends to cleanse each low desire;
Yet not at hazard is it sent,
The Saviour's eye is on us bent;
He's merciful, our truest friend,
Nor more than we require will send.
He's wise and prudent in his love,
Nor will the needed cross remove;
But when the evil is subdued,
And all the sinner's soul renewed,
Then may his every trial cease,
Then may his soul depart in peace;
For when the soul Christ's likeness shows,
Its fitness for himself he knows.
O to resemble him be mine,
To wake, and in his image shine!

In sorrow

When grieved by the coldness of those whom I love,
    To whom for relief shall I fly?
My Saviour, whom all my afflictions can move,
    He ever to cheer me is nigh.

Those whom I have cherished my friendship may scorn,
    My friends treat me, all, with contempt,
But he who for us of a virgin was born
    Was not from such evils exempt.

He came to his own, who received him not,
    His brethren believed not his word;
Ungrateful neglect was his desolate lot
    Who, of earth and of heaven, was Lord.

O thou! who to us an example hast left
    That we in thy footsteps should tread,
Of every delight in the creature bereft,
    To thy faithful arms I have fled.

There comfort and courage and wisdom I find,
    And every assistance I need;
Thy words on my heart as a girdle I bind,
    And from all distress I am freed.

Intercession

Christ! thou judge of quick and dead,
Thou who for my soul hast bled,
Thou in whom thy saints rejoice,
Listen to my pleading voice!

'Tis not for myself alone
I am bending at thy throne;
I would see thy grace extend
To the world's remotest end.

Now thy servants' labours crown.
Send thy Holy Spirit down,
And to every heathen land
Showers of heavenly light command.

For my native isle I pray,
May she share that glorious day,
All her stumbling-blocks remove,
Still rejoice her with thy love.

Long, thy mercies has she seen,
Long, thy favoured nation been;
By thine aid, hell's chain she broke,
Freed her from the papal yoke.

By thine aid, in later day
She repelled the tyrant's sway,
Guarded by thy matchless arm,
Safe she rode through all alarm.

Now, then, cast her not away,
In her greatest need, I pray,
But thy Holy Spirit pour
On her sons for evermore.

Thou, thy church's shield and rock,
Bless and keep thy little flock;
Guide them ever in the way,
Suffer not their feet to stray.

Let thy Spirit blessed be poured
On them in abundance, Lord,
May they by example bright,
Show the world thy glorious light.

Send choice blessings from above
Upon all the friends I love.
All good things unto them grant,
Satisfy their every want.

Chiefly, bless my parents dear,
Sanctify their hearts, and cheer;
Guide them in life's smoothest ways,
Guard and bless them all their days.

Keep my brothers, in their youth,
Firmly in the paths of truth;
May they youthful follies flee,
May their hearts be fixed on thee;

Till their mortal lives shall end,
Save, direct them and defend.
Whatsoever foes they meet
Tread thou underneath their feet!

Every relative I have,
I entreat thee, bless and save;
And may all who're kind to me
Be repaid ten-fold by thee.

Have I a malicious foe?
Have I such? I do not know.
I his injuries forgive.
Grant him grace to turn and live.

Let my prayers for all prevail
Who on mighty waters sail;
For the sick and the distressed,
That their trials may be blessed.

For the starving, wretched poor,
May they be oppressed no more!
For the prisoner in his cell,
Sighing for his native dell.

Grant to each a sure relief,
Suited to his several grief;
And may I most thankful be
All such woes are strange to me!

Lord, or e'er I cease to sing,
I would pray thee, bless our king.
Fostered by his reign of peace,
May our wealth and joys increase!

Lord, have mercy upon me,
Let me thy salvation see;
Cleanse me from each outward sin,
Make my heart all pure within.

I would but thy glory seek
In whate'er I do or speak,
Choose thy will and not my own,
Live to thee and thee alone.

Should our times be chequered o'er
With distress unknown before,
Should the church be sore oppressed,
Finding for her feet no rest;

Should it come to pass that might
Is esteemed undoubted right,
Should the troubled nations roar
Like a sea from shore to shore;

Should our nobles fall as stars,
Quenched in those disastrous wars;
Should the sun refuse his light,
And the moon be quenched in night;

Still in days as dark as those,
Thou art greater than our foes;
Still I hope thy praise to sing,
Borne as on the eagle's wing.

High things, Lord, I do not want,
Daily bread if thou wilt grant;
And my life to be my prey
Wheresoe'er I wandering stray.

When that night of woe is o'er,
Trouble then shall be no more.
Sad the eve, but fair the morn;
Night is darkest towards the dawn.

All life's griefs outweighed will be
If one hour that day I see.
Patiently I wait, O Lord,
Give me this for my reward!

Invocation to the Spirit

Spirit of truth and grace!
    Descend and live with me;
I have prepared a dwelling place
    Within my heart for thee.
Then do not, blessed one! delay
Thy coming, for a single day.

When thou, my hope, art come,
    Come ever to abide;
None else shall claim thy chosen home,
    'Twill own no Lord beside;
If thou to sojourn here wilt deign,
O'er all my thoughts and passions reign!

Spirit of truth and love!
    O hear me when I call!
I wait thy coming from above
    To be my king, my all.
Come to my heart! – it shall not be
Divided – it is all for thee!

Israel in the desert

When, by their Lord's command,
    Hasting to Canaan's land,
God's favoured race through burning deserts strayed,
    They wandered far and wide;
    Yet ever at their side
Flowed that deep stream which heat and thirst allayed.

They never needed bread,
    By heavenly manna fed,
Showered plenteously each morning from the sky;
    They did not, – could not know,
    The path they were to go,
Yet fearless walked, directed from on high;

And, all their wanderings past,
They safely reached at last,
That land of springs and vales, where honey flowed;
Nor upon Jordan's brink
With sorrow did they think
On all the dangers of their gone-by road.

Thus – may my life be led;
By God's free bounty fed,
May soul and body live secure from harm;
May waters from on high,
My spirit's thirst supply,
And Jesu's grace keep distant each alarm.

And when my failing breath,
Speaks the approach of death,
And I look back upon the path I've trod;
Then may I truly say,
"Though dark was oft my day,
Though devious the way,
'Twas the right path and led me to my God."

Lines in an old Bible

She, who first this book possessed
Long has been a spirit blessed!
'Mid earth's sorrows, toil, and strife,
By this book she ruled her life,
Till in heaven she proved its truth; –
Then 'twas sent to guide *my* youth.

'Twas in childhood my delight,
'Neath my pillow laid at night;
From its page my task I said,
In it to my parents read.
Thence I learnt in early youth,
To revere the God of truth.

Saviour! may its sacred page
Bless me through life's pilgrimage!
May I by the rules there given,
Pass each hour from hence to heaven;
And till death, still hold the truth
Which enlightened first my youth!

"Love your enemies"

Help me, my God, to love
    Those who do ill to me;
I seek thy grace from heaven above
    All angry thoughts to flee.

However much distressed
    With contradicting words,
Grant me, I pray, that perfect rest
    Trusting on thee affords.

And teach me Lord to see,
    However sorely tried,
That all thou dost is good for me,
    Should e'en the worst betide.

But grant, O grant, I pray,
    That nothing I endure
May tempt my soul from thee to stray
    E'en in the darkest hour!

But lest at last I fall,
    O'ercome by Satan's wiles,
O quit me not, my God, at all,
    And cheer me by thy smiles!

Missionary hymn

Fly ye swift messengers! O quickly fly!
Proclaim God's words of mercy from on high!
Bid all the heathen from their idols wake,
Bid all the guilty Satan's fetters break.
Tell the afflicted where to seek for aid,
Bid the meek-hearted be no more afraid,
Bid the transgressor fear his Master's rod;
Yea, bid the world prepare to meet their God!

For lo he cometh to avenge his cause!
O turn and tremble, ye who break his laws!
He comes to conquer for his saints, the earth,
To give his mourners peace and hallowed mirth,
To show his favour to the contrite soul,
Grace to exalt, and Satan to control;
Kings of the earth, O tremble at his rod,
Ye saints prepare, prepare to hail your God!

Then ye swift heralds of his mercy haste!
The holy city is a desert waste.
O bid your brethren rise and build her wall,
From highways, lanes and hedges bid them all;
The bridegroom cometh! let his spouse prepare;
The victor cometh! let his foes beware;
The judge is coming, sinners hear his rod!
Ye saints prepare to welcome back your God!

Missionary Prayer

O merciful God! may thy Spirit descend
　　On those who are striving sin's bondsmen to free;
Be thou to thy servants a parent and friend,
　　For parents and friends they have quitted for thee.

When to the deep waters their lives they commit,
　　Thou Lord who hast walked on the perilous wave,
Thou wilt not thy children in danger forget,
　　O let them not find in deep ocean a grave!

And when to the land of their banishment come,
    Preserve thou their lives, and their peace, and their health.
O! may they find joys in the far distant home
    More bright than life's honours, more rich than earth's wealth.

The sun is thy servant Lord, temper his rays,
    O shelter their heads from each pestilent blast!
Be love, faith and hope, the support of their days,
    And the bright crown of life their reward at the last.

O Spirit of grace! on their labours descend,
    And bless thou the seed which in weeping they sow
Do thou to the prayers of thy servants attend,
    And grant to the heathen their Saviour to know.

Yea bless Lord the men who so bravely go forth,
    And further their labours, and prosper thy cause,
Till the east and the west, and the south and the north,
    Believe in the Saviour and honour his laws.

Mutual Love

O 'tis a lovely thing to see,
When members of one family
In bonds of holy love agree,
    United in their Lord.

And 'tis a charming sound and sweet,
When friends around one altar meet
Each for the others to intreat
    To him who is their Lord.

And, better than ought else below,
Unto God's hallowed courts to go
With those whose kindred hearts, we know,
    Are worshipping the Lord.

O then what joy thy saints shall prove,
United in thy courts above,
To those, whom now on earth they love
    For thy dear sake, O Lord!

When to the great Redeemer's praise
Their voices they together raise,
Louder, more sweet, than seraph's lays,
    In honour of their Lord.

Be this, most gracious God, our end,
On earth from every harm defend,
And us thy little flock befriend,
    O holy God, our Lord!

And when the hour of death draws near
May Christian love our spirits cheer,
And thou thyself chase every fear
    From our last hours, O Lord!

And grant, O Saviour, I may see
All those on earth most dear to me
Joined to each other and to thee,
    And one in thee their Lord.

And when I reach the realms of light,
Grant me the infinite delight
To view them clad in robes of white,
    Made perfect in their Lord.

"No man can serve two masters"

And am I thine? Lord canst thou bear
    To dwell in hearts like mine?
In hearts presumptuous, that dare
To give the world so large a share
    Of what should all be thine.

How can I offer to my Lord
    A throne that rivals fill,
Nor buckle helmet on and sword,
And every needful aid afford
    Those hated foes to kill?

No man two lords at once can serve;
    And if the world and thou
Are rivals for my worthless love,
(The one so low, the one above
    All praises men bestow;)

Surely 'tis easy to decide
    Which master I should take.
The one will ever true abide
Whatever changes may betide.
    One will in woe forsake.

And yet that false and faithless friend,
    Can still engage the heart.
We know earth's joys in anguish end;
We know its paths to darkness tend;
    And yet we do not start.

We hope that we shall live to rue
    What we delight in now;
And so we phantoms false pursue;
But when their forms are lost to view,
    Then to the Lord we'll bow.

O, mad, and wicked, and perverse
    Who thus their conscience ease!
They hurry on from bad to worse,
And think thou wilt revoke thy curse
    Whenever they may please.

They seem as they'd a favour show,
    If e'er they choose to turn;
They sink their thoughts of God so low,
That in a while they hardly know
    Their deeds his vengeance earn.

O God, lest I should ever be
    Thus hardened by my sin,
At once from every ill I'll flee,
And do what's pleasing unto thee
    That I thy love may win.

O help me, these resolves to keep
   Whatever may befall,
That, if I wake, or if I sleep,
When I rejoice, and when I weep,
   I may be thine in all.

Of such is the kingdom of God

'Tis not the will of God Most High
  That one of these fair babes should die.
In heaven they see their Maker's face,
On earth they claim his care and grace.
Through ceaseless danger and alarm,
They pass, safe guarded by his arm.

When Christ our Lord was here below
He loved them all, as well we know.
He sharply chid his own beloved
When from his sight young babes they moved.
He kindly took them on his knee
And blessed them most lovingly.

If heaven you covet for your home,
He said, "You must as these become,
Be gentle as these babes, and mild,
To lowly things be reconciled.
They love their parents, so you must
Your heavenly Father love and trust.

To hurt these babes, if any dare,
My utmost vengeance he shall share;
'Twere better he were never born
Than thus his Maker's will to scorn;
For truly he my wrath shall see
Who useth them untenderly,

But punishment that has no end
Is theirs who cause them to offend,
They, who their tender minds pervert,
And teach them what their souls will hurt,
Themselves shall sink in error's ways,
And end in misery their days.

But nothing you can do or say,
In their behalf, is thrown away;
If you a cup of water give,
A recompense you shall receive;
And when my gentle lambs you feed,
I have your payment full decreed."

Thou wouldst not then, O Lord Most High,
That one of these thy babes should die;
Thou hast commanded me to teach
Thy sacred words to all and each;
Then surely Lord thou dost intend
Thyself to stand my children's friend.

Thou biddest me to teach and pray,
Thou bidd'st me watch them night and day,
And guard their minds from every ill;
Then wilt thou not *thy* part fulfil,
And every hurtful weed remove
That checks the growth of heavenly love?

And wilt thou not thine aid extend,
To me their guardian and their friend?
O teach me all I ought to say!
Improve my judgment day by day!
Increase my love, my labours bless,
And crown them with complete success!

On a child's death

Lord hast thou set a mark
Upon thy children's brow?
A mark of heavenly birth
Whereby the world may know
That those so humble in their eyes
Are kings and angels in disguise?

Ah! little did I know
What the sweet charm could be
That bound my secret heart
Fair stranger unto thee.
Now feel I, 'twas thy filial love
To him who reigns supreme above.

But thou art flown away;
No more we see thy face.
Thou wast not fit for earth;
Heaven is thy proper place.
Thou did for angels' converse long,
And now thy praises swell their song!

Thou, in life's earliest spring,
Ere others seed is sown,
Wast like bright autumn's day,
Thy harvest ripe had grown.
No need of summer's scorching heat
To make thee for the garner meet!

The God who heareth prayer
Bent down his ear to thine;
"Lord take my soul away
In thy bright courts to shine;
I long, my God, to fly to thee;
Let me a beauteous angel be."

These were the simple words
Which thou one morn hadst said;
Christ heard the prayer of faith,
Nor answer long delayed,
Thy Saviour came that very night,
And made his child a saint in light!

And shall we mourn thee? No!
We do thee not such wrong;
We envy thee, sweet boy,
We sigh to join thy song;
We tremble lest, earth's troubles past,
We fail to share thy bliss at last!

On a little girl's birthday

O look in kindness, Lord, on all
    My youthful friends, I pray;
But chiefly shower thy grace on her
    Whose birthday is today.

I thank thee for her life preserved,
    For health and sense possessed,
And every other precious gift
    Wherewith her life is blessed.

O may she have a thankful heart
    To praise thy name for all;
And give her patience and content
    When trials shall befall.

Extend, Lord, still thy guarding hand,
    And guide her through the year;
O may thy word each passing day
    Her path direct and cheer.

May she most earnestly resolve,
    Supported by thy grace,
To enter, by faith's narrow door,
    The paths of heavenly peace.

And, O my God, instruct me how
    To feed her infant soul;
How lead her in religion's ways,
    How best her heart control.

And may she, guarded by thy shield,
    Escape from Satan's snares,
And with the Spirit's sword, attack,
    And foil his wiles by prayers.

Thus ever led and helped by thee,
    Her Saviour and her God,
May she approach from day to day
    More near thy blest abode,

Until at length her ransomed soul,
    Veiled by the flesh no more,
From all defilement cleansed and free,
    To meet her God shall soar.

There may she find all loved on earth
    To part no more again;
There in the sunbeam of thy smiles,
    For ever glad remain!

On some children, saying their prayers

The room is hushed, I look, and view around
My little ones, all kneeling on the ground;
Though still each voice, he who can secrets read,
He knows whose hearts are raised to him indeed.
O! be their infant spirits upward drawn
When thus they worship God at eve and morn,
And be their prayers to heaven by angels borne.

"Where two or three are met to worship me,
    Amidst them shall my presence ever be,"
Saith Christ – and often, when I'm standing by,
I think with joy, yet awe, – the Saviour's nigh,
Are solemn thoughts at such a season meet?
Then, surely, solemn blessings I intreat
For those I see thus kneeling at his feet.

O thou that hearest prayer! canst thou refuse
As thine own children these my babes to choose?
They all are children of a thousand prayers,
Anxieties and heaven-directed cares;
O! hearken, Lord, to their requests and mine;
Thou Sun of righteousness! upon them shine,
And own them now, – and evermore, as thine?

Praise for God's mercies

O give me Lord a grateful heart
    For all thou dost bestow;
And may that heart be fixed on thee
    From whom my blessings flow!

Thy gifts I prize; O, is not then
    The Giver doubly dear?
Should all thy gifts at once depart,
    I'm rich if thou art near.

Lord, ever merciful and kind,
    Teach me to sing thy praise
Not only with my lips, – to thee
    I consecrate my days.

And if long life thou give, – that life
    Shall unto thee be given;
And if I early die, – much more
    I'll sing thy praise in heaven.

I'm in thy hands to do with me
 As shall to thee seem best;
But fit me more and more each day
 For everlasting rest.

Prayer for a happy death

Lord! let me die the righteous' death,
 Yea, be my end like his!
Who humbly trusts, his last drawn breath,
 Begins eternal bliss.

How often has my inmost heart
 In secret breathed this prayer,
When reading how thy saints depart
 Without a fear or care.

But when upon their death I muse,
 To view their lives I turn;
For I, if their calm end I choose,
 To act like them must learn,

Saviour! the lives of holy men,
 When I their story read,
Rouse up my failing faith again
 To pray and strive indeed.

Then if from sinners' lives we gain
 Instruction so divine,
What wisdom shall we not obtain
 By daily studying thine!

Prayer for forgiveness

Conducted by thy staff and rod
Through this my pilgrim life, O God,
By thy permission, thy command,
To beg forgiveness, here I stand.

Thou didst for mine offences bleed,
Forgive them all by word or deed;
O cast into the unfathomed sea
My sins and mine iniquity!

My sins by thought more heinous yet,
Not only pardon but forget;
Lord hide them as behind a cloud,
With a thick veil my errors shroud!

My Saviour! in thy name I plead
From sin's defilement to be freed;
To each good purpose give thou strength,
And grant full victory at length!

Prayer for patience

Come heavenly patience! be my stay
When hope's bright visions fade away,
And disappointment's clouds instead
Are darkly lowering o'er my head.

Can it be chance that ever blights
Our schemes of joy, our hoped delights,
That pictures bliss in colours fair,
But grasp it, and it melts to air?

Chance! no 'tis providence divine,
Who wills we earthly joys resign,
And by these painful lessons says,
"Christian to heaven thy wishes raise!"

O hard 'tis for the wilful soul,
Unused her wishes to control,
To bid the Lord do what he will,
And be resigned and happy still!

Teach *me* by prayer and meditation,
Dear Lord, to feel this resignation;
And when earth's griefs my heart oppress,
In thee to find all happiness.

Ah, yes; may that blessed frame be mine,
Which says to thee, "I all resign;
Thy will, my God, I choose alone,
For good or evil, be it done!"

Prayer for peace

Source of all wisdom! lo I kneel,
    A suppliant for thy grace;
Thou whose instructions make me feel
My ignorance; – more light reveal,
    And guide me into peace!

Peace, Lord, I seek; but here below
    How many things there are
That make life's stream ungently flow,
That change our joys to bitter woe,
    And kindle strife and war.

A "peace-maker"! O title blest!
    May I such title claim;
Search all the lands from east to west,
Where, without peace, is joy or rest?
    Be "peace-maker" my name!

But that true peace I may enjoy,
    Make me both just and wise,
Nor, lest their quarrels me annoy,
Neglect authority t'employ,
    O'er those who rule despise,

And may the wars and scenes of strife
    With which all lands abound,
Wean my affections from this life,
Which is with such distresses rife
    That rest can ne'er be found.

I hear thy voice, "Arise! depart!"
    And joyfully obey;
Thou hast already claimed my heart;
With all else willingly I part,
    And hasten on my way.

Yet is this earth to mortals dear,
    And God, who knows 'tis so,
Has promised days of quiet here,
Days which faith's eye e'en now sees near,
    When earth shall sabbaths know.

"O! speed them Lord!" my spirit cries!
    Like Simeon, may I see,
Before I close my weary eyes,
The Sun of that fair morn arise;
    Then welcome death to me!

Prayer for the Jews

Lord! for Jerusalem we'll pray,
Nor give thee rest by night or day
    Until thou do her bless;
Our tears for her rebellion flow,
We think with pity on her woe,
    And all her sins confess.

We read the promise in thy book,
And then upon her stones we look,
    All scattered in the dust;
We daily pray for Zion's peace;
That all her troubles soon shall cease
    We confidently trust.

She long denied her Saviour-God,
And long has writhed beneath the rod
    Her unbelief procured;
But now, O let thy wrath depart,
And take away her stony heart,
    For much she hath endured.

Unto her mourners peace restore,
O comfort her for evermore!
    'Tis time Lord to begin;
Her sister church, the Gentiles, pray
That thou wilt give without delay
    A pardon for her sin.

For when thy promise is fulfilled,
And thou again wilt Salem build,
    And all thy glory show;
The heathen then shall fear thy name,
And distant kings thy power proclaim
    Which all the earth shall know.

Thus when we for the Hebrews pray,
We hope that we, as well as they,
    Shall joyful answer gain;
O Lord! prolong our lives to see
All nations reconciled to thee,
    Thine ever to remain!

Preparation

Lord, while peace thou dost bestow,
Help me to prepare for woe!
May I hear thy warning call
Bidding me sit loose on all
This most changing world can give
In the few short years I live.

While youth's pleasures still engage,
Help me to prepare for age!
Laying up, from day to day,
Wealth that cannot flee away,
Faith, humility and love,
Current gold in heaven above.

While in health I still remain
Fit me for the bed of pain !
Grant O Lord that I may learn
Suffering into good to turn.
Thus each hour of life, may I
Be preparing, Lord, to die.

Repentance

My God, in shame and grief extreme,
    I bow before thy throne;
Thou knowest what my sins have been,
    Thou knowest, thou alone;
How could I ever, Lord, consent,
To do what now I so repent?

How little, even yet, I know
    The vileness of my heart;
Though wearied of all things below
    I yet from thee depart;
I love thee more than all beside,
And yet forsake thee when I'm tried.

My sin is known to none but thee.
    I would have rather died
Than that a fellow worm should see
    My thoughts; – but can I hide,
However dark the favouring night,
The smallest action from thy sight?

Yet may be not alone the Lord,
    My guilty conscience knows;
For we have notice in his word
    That angels watch o'er those
Who trust in Christ's atoning blood,
And dedicate themselves to God.

And shall I their protection crave,
    Then scare them by my sin?
And when such guardians pure I have,
    Dare I let Satan in?
I wonder at my sins, O God!
How can I thus provoke thy rod?

And, Oh! when that great day shall come,
    When all things now concealed
Shall, ere the Judge pronounce my doom,
    Be to the world revealed;
How shall I bear, that all I've done
Should to my fellow men be known?

The human heart, when it is best
    Is quite unworthy thee;
But mine has been a very nest
    Of all iniquity;
If kept from outward wickedness,
To thee alone the glory is.

E'en now, I would not dare to say
    I will offend no more;
I can but for forgiveness pray,
    And constant help implore.
If I should think to promise, Lord,
How couldst thou now believe my word?

But Oh! I humbly would intreat,
    That all my present pain,
May teach me that, though sin be sweet,
    Its end is worse than vain;
Ne'er may it, now I've felt its sting,
My soul again to bondage bring.

To thee once more I yield my heart;
    Guard it by night and day;
At sin's appearance may I start,
    And quickly turn away;
Thus from the tempter's wiles defend,
And guard me till my life shall end,

Repentance

O God! it is not to be borne,
    This painful sense of sin;
I cannot rest, for thee I mourn,
    And all is dark within;
'Tis just the heart should pine and smart,
That from its Saviour could depart.

But O, forsake me not I pray;
    But to my guilty soul
Grant strength to turn no more away,
    And do thou make me whole;
My soul release! Restore my peace!
And may my joy in thee increase!

If even all the world were mine,
    And sure for countless years,
It were not worth a smile of thine
    To chase my griefs and fears;
O then I pray, "Turn not away,
Nor leave me sad again today."

Thou say'st that those who wait for thee
    Shall thy salvation view;
The mercies which thy servants see
    Are every morning new;
They are, I know; I've felt them so;
But now my portion is but woe.

Thou wilt that I should know and feel
    Sin's bitterness of pain;
But now, O turn thou, and reveal
    Thy wonted grace again,
Nought else to me can ever be
A joy, if loved no more by thee!

The idol cause of all my grief
    I willingly resign,
Of my offending 'tis the chief.
    Though loved, I'll not repine,
But from me cast all follies past
Nor keep back this, the first and last.

Self-dedication

"Christ's to suffer and to serve,"
How can I the name deserve?
Dearest Lord, behold thou me,
Bound for life to work for thee!

Use my tongue, my hands, my feet;
Use my heart while that shall beat;
Use my purse, its gold is thine,
Use whatever else is mine.

Lord whate'er thou wilt, I will;
Give me faith and patience still.
This bright name may I deserve,
Thine to suffer and to serve!

Self-knowledge

Who can understand his heart?
Lord to all this grace impart,
That we may more clearly know
Whence our sins and trials flow.

Who would guess the depths of sin
Till he should this search begin? –
Who can e'er be proud again?
Who such knowledge shall obtain?

Christian, now begin to look
In this all-important book,
And resolve that what you learn
You'll forthwith to practice turn.

But in vain you on it pore,
You're no better than before;
Faults you see, faults without end,
Easier 'tis to find than mend.

Will you yield to dark despair,
Beat the breast, the garments tear?
Will you give the study o'er,
And distress the mind no more?

Well you might to sadness yield
Were no hope for man revealed;
Well you might your efforts end
Did success on you depend.

But, O man, it is not so,
None are doomed to hopeless woe;
None are bid to seek in vain,
None need hopelessly complain.

Means of learning simple are,
God's own book, and earnest prayer,
This is all the lore you need;
Having this, you're wise indeed.

Read that book, and you will view
All that God requires of you;
Read, and you in time will find
Why you are so ill inclined,

How, and wherefore, you offend,
How your steps to darkness tend;
How unworthy of the skies,
How unable to arise.

There you'll learn how Jesus died,
And your righteousness supplied;
And rich grace that he will give
To assist you how to live;

And you'll learn by searching there
All the benefits of prayer,
What the wonders it achieves,
What the strength man thence receives.

When you've tried this simple plan,
Soon you'll be an altered man;
Then once more your heart consult,
And how different the result.

You may still have cause to mourn,
It so little fruit has borne;
Sometimes evil may prevail,
Or your best intentions fail.

But th'affections all are changed,
And in virtue's service ranged;
Sins which gave you once delight,
Now are hateful in your sight.

No more proud and scornful now,
Calm but modest is your brow;
He who heavenward humbly walks,
Meekly to his fellows talks.

Churlish to the poor no more,
Wide you ope your friendly door;
And where'er the glad rejoice
There is heard your cheerful voice.

Every other Christian grace,
Now assumes its proper place,
Proving, though you walk the earth,
You from Heaven derive your birth.

Thus the Christian ought to live,
Grace for this will Jesus give;
Make it but your constant care,
These are all the fruits of prayer!

"Strong in the Lord"

Thou heardest Lord my solemn vow
    All idols to forsake;
I would renew that promise now,
    And thee my witness make;

But not in my own strength alone
    Resolve I to amend,
Thou art my strength, Almighty One!
    My helper and my friend.

'Tis by thy grace alone I stand
    If I to stand attain;
And when I break thy just command,
    By that I rise again.

I now intreat that grace, O Lord,
    My promises to keep;
Thou hast engaged thy help t'afford,
    And lead thy erring sheep.

Without thee I am weak and poor,
    Aided by thee I'm strong;
Impart thy strength now evermore
    To keep me safe from wrong.

"Suffer the little children to come unto me"

Lord, thou hast made the infant race
    Thine own peculiar care;
In heaven they all behold thy face,
    Types of thy saints they are.

Those who to them a favour show,
      By thee shall be repaid;
Those who offend and cause them woe,
      On them thy curse is laid.

These gracious words my fears remove,
      Yea, make my hope abound,
That all the children that I love
      Have thy protection found.

Prosper my care and labour, Lord,
      To make them seek thy face;
A blessing on my words afford,
      And may they grow in grace.

For those, thou wilt rewards prepare,
      Who ought to them have given,
O then be mine, for this my care,
      To meet them all in heaven!

Sunday evening

Forgive me, Lord, my wandering thoughts
      This day before thy throne;
My folly and my heedlessness
      To thee too well are known.

I went into thy house, resolved
      To pray with all my heart,
That, blest and strengthened, to my home
      I might in peace depart.

But foolish thoughts, by Satan breathed,
      Stole my light heart away,
And small advantage 'twas, alas,
      That I knelt down to pray.

Forgive me, Father, now, and grant
      This time may be the last
That I forgot I came to pray
      Until prayer time is past.

Sunday hymn

O well I love the sacred day
   On which my Saviour rose!
Like him, at morning's earliest ray,
I'll fling sleep's death-like coils away,
   And cast aside earth's woes.

Dear is the day, most dear, to me!
   How sweet it is to raise,
Kind Lord, our suppliant hands to thee,
Sweet to adore thy majesty
   In rude but heart-felt lays!

How sweet to hear the gospel news
   From fervent lips proclaimed;
Who then obedience could refuse?
O who to hearken would not choose,
   When Christ is fondly named?

But sweetest, at the sacred board,
   It is with faith to kneel;
O! when we hear the thrilling word
"Eat in remembrance of thy Lord!"
   Who does not ardour feel?

"For thy Redeemer, Saviour's sake,
   Who shed his blood for thee,
This cup we bless, this bread we break,
And bid thee in remembrance take
   Of his dread agony."

And shall his servants bid in vain
   To such a rich repast?
Yea, shall they call and call again,
To those he saved from endless pain;
   And will they choose to fast?

No! sweet God's public service is,
   And sweet, prayer's lonely breath;
But yet a dearer, warmer bliss,
My soul hath felt, and it is this,
   To celebrate his death!

Sunday morning

Sweet day of heavenly rest!
Thee choose and love I best
In all the seasons of the changeful year;
    But at this glorious time,
    Bright summer in her prime
Decks thee with charms that make thee fair as dear.

    As day's bright Lord awakes,
    And the dim stillness breaks,
Chasing night's shadows with a conqueror's power;
    Then, ere he drinketh up
    Dews from each floweret's cup,
I love to walk – 'tis thought's most favoured hour.

    It is not idle rest
    That pleases me the best,
Not indolence indulged in slothful bed;
    When in each bower and brake,
    Heaven's choristers awake,
They warble near me till my dreams are fled.

    And great is my delight,
    On Sabbath mornings bright,
To drink sweet draughts of dawn's reviving air;
    Unenviously I hear
    The sounds of slumberers near,
I leave them all, and seek the garden fair.

    In that beloved retreat,
    Beauties unnumbered meet
My raptured eyes, and sweets my senses fill,
    Whilst in the air there wake
    Sounds that low music make
Of bird, and rustling breeze, and rippling rill.

Now, falling on mine ear,
    Soft distant sounds I hear,
'Tis the loved lesson of the village bell!
    "Christian", it says, "prepare;
    Of Sabbath sins beware;
Come here today, and flee the paths of hell,"

"Ye who count heaven your home,
    No need to bid *you* come,
Ye hungering souls! to ask your weekly food;
    Ye who the evil know,
    Of want, and pain, and woe,
Come, and entreat the source of every good!

"Ye, whose abundant wealth,
    And joy, and youth, and health,
Tempt you to fix too much your hearts on earth,
    Come and your Maker praise,
    And learn your souls to raise
Towards Him who giveth blessings far more worth."

Thus seems the bell to call
    On each of us, and all,
And bids us haste, and our devotions pay:
    O may we all delight,
    And in God's courts unite
To spend in hallowed rest the sacred day.

Moments, ye fly too fast!
    My morning walk is past,
Again I turn me to the haunts of man;
    Leisure no more is mine,
    Yet do I not repine,
But rather seize its blessings when I can.

My offerings today
    I shall more purely pay
For this soft hour of meditative rest;
    The truths thy servants teach,
    My inmost soul shall reach
The rather that my thoughts have been so blest.

And grant thou, Lord, I pray,
　That all this blessed day
May with its peaceful dawning well agree;
　Each thought, and act, and word,
　On this thy Sabbath, Lord,
I would devote to piety and thee!

Thanksgiving

Thanks to thee, for every blessing
　Which thy bounteous hand bestows!
O the joy, Lord, of confessing
　Whence my smallest comfort flows!

Thanks for every changing season!
　All are ordered thus by thee;
Thanks for youth and health and reason,
　All that make life sweet to me!

Thanks for day's serene employments,
　And for peaceful eve's repose;
For these leisure hours' enjoyments,
　When my daily duties close.

For the glow of healthful pleasure
　Which through all my senses thrills;
For content, man's greatest treasure,
　Which my life with gladness fills.

Thanks for every precious token
　Thou hast given of love to me;
Thanks for every promise spoken
　To thy servants, Lord, by thee!

At thy mercy seat when kneeling,
　Praying, from my sins relief,
Thanks for every spark of feeling,
　For a heart bowed low with grief.

Thanks for every glimpse of heaven
  Through life's clouds discerned afar;
Thanks for every triumph given
  In this world's unceasing war.

Much I love, O Lord, confessing,
  Whence my every comfort flows.
Still then shower on me each blessing
  Which thy kindness now bestows.

Thanksgiving

Thanks to thee, who dost bestow
All the happiness I know,
And with hope dost cheer the way,
Soon to end in cloudless day.

Thanks to thee who dost impart
Heavenly knowledge to my heart;
Love to warm it, – faith to guide,
Whatsoever may betide.

Thanks, eternal thanks, to thee
Who hast shed thy blood for me;
This, of all thy gifts the best,
Crowns and sanctifies the rest.

Thanksgiving for peace

I thank thee, gracious Lord,
Who hast my peace restored,
  And chased the clouds of woe;
For every peaceful day
My thanks to thee I pay,
  Who dost all good bestow.

I raise my hopes above
To those fair realms of love
    Where nought but peace is known;
For greatly do I fear,
The peace I've sought for here
    Will soon be lost and gone.

Of peace I often sing,
It is the only thing
    I eagerly desire;
My peace do thou increase,
Thou lovely Prince of Peace,
    Who didst the wish inspire!

The Saviour's testament
Was peace that should be sent
    To those who loved their Lord;
Peace, that should ever last,
Despite the world's cold blast,
    Despite the heathen's sword.

O may this peace be mine,
For ours is all that's thine;
    Lord, magnify thy name!
Amid the tears and strife
Of this my pilgrim life,
    My heritage I claim!

The Beatitudes

Blessed are the poor in spirit,
They, heaven's kingdom shall inherit;
Bless'd who bow to sorrow's rod,
They shall comfort find from God;
Surely too the meek are bless'd,
By them earth shall be possess'd;
Bless'd who seek celestial food,
God shall fill their souls with good,
Bless'd are they who mercy show,
Heaven's compassion shall they know;
Bless'd whose hearts are cleansed by grace,
They shall see the Maker's face;
Bless'd are they who peace proclaim,
God's own children is their name;
Blessed they who suffer ill
While they seek their Master's will;
Made for them my kingdom is,
They shall be the heirs of bliss!
Blessed, whosoe'er ye be,
Who endure distress for me;
When mankind your names shall curse,
Treating you now ill, now worse,
Great your recompense shall be,
If you thus endure for me;
I will needful strength supply;
Bravely, like the Prophets, die!

The Bees

Hark to that sound!
   'Tis the humming of bees,
Swarming around
   The ancient lime trees!

Each morning betimes
   I seek the fresh air,
But those merry chimes
   Are heard earlier there!

I walk in the eve
   Of the sultry day,
My tasks glad to leave, –
   But not so they.

At dawn's first peep
   Is their work begun,
At their toil they keep,
   Till the setting sun.

Like them would I strive,
   In youth's sunny spring,
So wisely to live
   That when winter shall fling

His cold arms around me,
   I smiling may say,
"Well stored hast thou found me,
   I fear not thy sway!"

The benefits of prayer

O talk not of prayer as a task to be done
In the wearisome race we, though wearied, must run,
As duty returning with morning and night,
Which still must be practised, because it is right.

O never thus speak, of the Christian's best treasure!
In business, his aid, his employment in leisure,
His guide when perplexed, his first refuge in sorrow,
His food for today, and his hope for the morrow.

O where should we flee to escape from despair,
If forbidden to pour out our sorrows in prayer?
How should we find strength from temptation to fly?
How ill should we live, O how wretchedly die!

All blessings are ours, God's gift in his Son,
But how without prayer shall these blessings be won?
The Spirit is ours, poured on us from heaven,
By asking 'tis found, to the kneeling 'tis given.

To the sick it is medicine, and streams to the faint,
The sinner's first hope, the last breath of the saint,
'Tis the bond that unites all the church to its Head,
The manna by which all God's children are fed.

When burdened with guilt, 'tis our only relief,
It easeth all pain, and it soothes every grief;
It guideth our steps till we enter the skies,
And all we can need on life's journey, supplies.

Speak not then of prayer as of task to be done,
But call it the sword whereby vict'ry is won,
O call it the treasure by Christians possessed,
The key of heaven's store-house, the pledge of heaven's rest.

The lily of the valley

Ah! see the first-born lily of the year
    Blown but this hour!
Why is the lily to my heart more dear
    Than any flower?

Why does my spirit feel a softened joy
    To see it blow?
Why do I thus my time and care employ
    To seek it low?

Because it ever bringeth to my mind
    One whom I love;
One who is, – though his emblems low I find,
    Highest above.

Why do I call this humble floweret then
    Type of my God,
E'en though he once with us unholy men
    As man abode?

Than Adam's race more fair, far brighter *He*,
    In virtue ripe!
Would not the stately oak, or cedar, be
    His fitter type?

Nay, let himself decide, hear his own word!
   "Ye poor, draw nigh,
And follow me, your meek and humble Lord,
   For poor am I.

"And they who follow me, in heart are poor.
   And lowly, all;
To such alone I ope heaven's friendly door,
   Them, brethren call."

Then must the lily of the valley be
   His type in truth,
Like him, its blossoms meekly bent, we see
   From earliest youth.

Unnoticed, near the earth it hidden lies,
   Unknown, forgot;
Save where the heart directs our anxious eyes
   To find the spot.

If 'mid earth's myriads, He alone was pure
   From all offence,
This spotless lily shows, in image sure,
   His innocence.

If fragrance be the lily's attribute,
   Scenting the air!
Him, it resembleth then without dispute,
   As sweet as fair!

Thus if the lily pleases me above
   All flowers that be,
'Tis that it telleth most of him I love,
   Who loveth me.

More pure, more sweet, and meeker far, He is,
   Than this pale weed.
He who may call the peerless lily his
   Is rich indeed!

As in a mirror bright, then, let us view
    Our Saviour's face,
That we may know, and learn to copy too,
    His every grace,

And when we gaze upon these gentle flowers
    Which charm our sight,
We'll seek to make thy lowly virtue ours,
    O Lord of light!

Be ours to imitate thy graces now
    That, coming down,
Thou may us pluck to wreathe thy royal brow,
    A living crown!

The lonely missionary's soliloquy

Can it be good, Lord, for thy sheep
At distance from the fold to keep?
Can it be good to dwell afar
From where the folds and shepherds are?

'Tis often good to be alone,
To muse; – and plead before thy throne;
But, ever to continue thus,
Can this, dear Lord, be good for us?

Alone Thou bidd'st thy children dwell
Apart from those who tend to hell;
But from each other must they be?
Can that be pleasing, Lord, to thee?

Though fainting, – me no shepherd feeds,
No hand to living waters leads; –
A wandering sheep that none will seek,
Alone and desolate and weak!

Is this thy will concerning me?
Can this Lord for thy glory be?
It is! O yes, it must be so!
Teach me thy purposes to know!

"O be thou cleansed," saith thy word,
"Who bear the vessels of the Lord!"
O make me clean that I too, may,
The light of life to all display.

Salt, to a lost corrupted earth,
Food to a land of grievous dearth,
Guides to direct the wanderer lone,
These dost thou bid thy flock become.

But did they all together live,
How could they this assistance give?
But thou hast scattered them abroad
That they may light the world to God.

Be this thy purpose, Lord, towards me,
Dispenser of thy grace to be,
A voice the slumbering to awake,
A guide to those who sin forsake!

O be it thus! my life control!
Awake, refresh, and cleanse my soul!
Though sin entice on every side,
Still grant me faithful to abide.

Do thou my fainting soul restore,
And shepherds will I seek no more;
The shepherd's Shepherd Lord thou art,
And all thy flock are near thy heart.

We think ourselves alone, but oh!
While thou art near it is not so;
At hand thou art to guide and tend,
And feed and cheer us to the end.

Then fears and haltings hence, begone,
From henceforth I am not alone,
Were all earth mine, I should not be
So blessed as when I walk with thee.

The missionary's reward

What is the blessing *they* receive,
    E'en in this present time,
Who friends and home and comfort leave,
    And seek some distant clime,
And brave contempt, disease, and shame,
So they may honour Jesus' name?

'Twere easy, sure, their loss to tell,
    In all that men hold dear,
The parents, brethren, loved so well,
    Whose smiles their toil would cheer,
Life's social joys, their Christian friends.
What for such loss can make amends?

Yet, "in this present time," He saith,
    And not alone in heaven,
Shall unto these meek sons of faith
    A hundredfold be given;
What can the gifts be that atone
For living poor, distressed, alone?

The peace of heaven, God's tender love,
    Support in toils and cares,
The Spirit's graces from above,
    Christ's mediatorial prayers,
Of these, how large a share they claim
Who quit their all for Jesus' name.

And then the joy, the sweet delight,
    When years of care are past,
To view their flock, from sin's dark night,
    Awake to God at last;
And hear them till their latest breath,
Bless him who saved their souls from death.

O yes! if no peculiar crown
   Awaited such in heaven,
Reward sufficient, theirs alone,
   To them on earth is given;
Yes, for each earthly joy they leave
A hundredfold they here receive!

The mother's care

Delightful, says the poet, is the task
To guide the soft and pliant mind of youth,
To implant the germs of wisdom in their hearts,
To lead them step by step from childhood, up
To youth and manhood. – But the bard spoke not
From knowledge by his own experience gained,
But as a poet guessed. What could he know
Of all the fears, and griefs, and tender cares
The trembling mother feels? – by love of God
And of her offspring, rendered wise as fond,
Thoughtful and prudent, diligent and grave;
Who seeks, with anxious beating heart, a proof,
However faint, that God her work has owned;
Who loves with more than mother's love, and fears
Where common parents sleep; who says, "this child
I lend to God," and that her infant should
The covenant confirm is all her hope.
Think if her child the tender care repay
With dull indifference, or wayward pride,
And spurn the guidance of her gentle hand,
And pay her love with selfish cold contempt,
As I have known, alas! – Surely the curse
"Write this man childless," were a happy lot
Compared with hers. – Great Father of the world,
Look kindly on my babes! O call them thine;
And when before thy judgment-seat we stand,
Grant me, to say – "Behold, Lord, here I am,
And with me all the children of my love;
Thy gift they were, I brought them up for thee,
And now, behold them all, at thy right hand!

The Preacher

God saw his single-minded heart,
    God marked his fervent zeal;
And grace unfettered did impart
    The lost to save and heal.

With his great Master for his type
    He issued forth to teach;
Tears from the streaming eye to wipe,
    Hope to the lost to preach.

His pulpit floor, the springing grass,
    His walls, the clustering trees,
His auditor, whoe'er may pass,
    His flock, whome'er he sees;

His chapel roof, the clouded sky,
    His notebook, God's own word,
His licence, love to men who die,
    And zeal to serve their Lord.

Thus fled full many a year away;
    Nor purpose did he know
Than seeking every night and day
    His Saviour's will to do.

He died; – but at the day of doom
    Ten thousands shall we see
Who learned to flee the wrath to come
    From him, and such as he.

And do we wish the throng to swell?
    Their perfect bliss to share?
Yea, would we with those saved ones dwell
    Whom here we cannot bear?

Yes! then since we would meet in heaven,
    May we to scorn them fear;
And let us pray that grace be given,
    To love as brethren here.

We may not, – need not, quite agree
　　In all that we believe;
Yet but one Lord, both they and we,
　　One rule of life receive.

One only parent had we all
　　By whose one sin we fell;
By the same law we stand or fall,
　　On the same earth we dwell.

To the same Maker owe our birth,
　　To the same stroke our death,
Lie in the self-same damp dark earth,
　　From the same air draw breath.

At the same throne of grace we kneel,
　　We all forgiveness need;
The Spirit's same assistance feel,
　　On heaven's same manna feed.

Then let us 'neath one banner fight,
　　And join in cordial love,
That as old friends we may unite
　　When we shall meet above.

For there, nor heresy shall be,
　　Nor other cause of strife;
Faith shall be lost when God we see,
　　And hope in endless life.

Here we must patiently endure.
　　And mutual failings bear;
But heaven shall every difference cure,
　　For perfect peace dwells there!

The Snowdrop

Ah! little do you know, dear child,
　　How ill your words apply,
When you compare this lovely flower
　　To such a one as I!

This flower, (while I deep sunk in guilt,
    Was sinful from my birth)
Rose from her dark and miry tomb,
    Untinged by stain of earth.

While I, 'mid blessings numberless,
    Unthankful, fruitless, live,
This fair one, to the wintry skies,
    Her best array doth give.

While ever she her timid face
    Turns meekly to the ground,
How oft, for happiness, do I,
    Unsated, look around!

Oh how unlike, then! are we not?
    It seems like mockery
To hear the snowdrop pure compared,
    Though e'en in jest, to me.

And yet, my love, although your type
    Suits now, nor you, nor me,
I feign will hope the hour may come
    When we as pure may be.

Few days have passed since this sweet flower
    Was as we all now are;
Earth held it, soiled its humble form,
    And hid its beauties rare.

But suns unseen, its life renewed,
    On rains scarce felt, it fed,
Till, fitted for a purer life,
    It spurned its lowly bed.

On us too, heavenly dews distilled:
    The Holy Spirit rains,
And Jesu's blood shed all for us,
    Shall wash our earthly stains.

The sun of grace and righteousness
   Shall cheer each mourning heart,
And hallowed fear, and filial love,
   And holiness, impart.

Though hidden now, these graces droop,
   And blush for sin's deep soil;
O think how soon they shall throw off
   Corruption's hateful coil!

How soon, in robes as stainless white,
   Our souls may be arrayed,
And our glad brows, enwreathed with flowers,
   Heaven's flowers, that never fade!

Till then, to nought so pure, may we
   Our sinful hearts compare;
But, knowing not what we shall be,
   Lament for what we are!

"There is none upon earth I desire in comparison of thee"

Although I've not all earthly bliss,
   Yet why should I repine,
No human joys could equal this,
   To know that Christ is mine.

No friend is near, no parent kind,
   To charm away my fears;
No kindly sympathy I find
   To dry my falling tears;

And be it so, – for one there is,
   Than brother dearer far,
Who deigns to claim my heart as his,
   His, my affections are.

My every grief he charms away,
   My every step attends;
His eye upon me night and day
   In anxious love he bends.

The world despises and forsakes;
    Then Jesus nearer draws.
The world, perhaps, advantage takes,
    But he will plead my cause.

He seeth not as mortals see,
    They to appearance look;
But by the heart decideth he,
    Who ne'er his own forsook.

Let others then of beauty boast,
    Of honours, wealth and friends;
But I, possessing Christ, have most,
    Whose kindness never ends.

Now in my youth I'll call him mine,
    To latest age he'll bear;
Whate'er my lot, I'll not repine,
    But cast on him my care.

"This is not your rest"

This world seems but a dreary waste,
    To those, who homeward bound,
Long, the sweet fruits of heaven to taste,
    And be with victory crowned.

To those who boast a better home,
    How wearisome is earth!
Uncharmed by wordly joys *they* roam,
    Who claim a heavenly birth.

The joys that in life's desert grow,
    They trust not, though they taste;
Knowing they from God's mercy flow,
    They take, then pass in haste.

Whatever good the world affords
    Is but a type of heaven.
He uses not aright, who hoards,
    What was but lent, not given.

We would not all life's joy condemn,
   Nor make it yet our god;
That seems God's favours to contemn,
   While *this* provokes his rod,

But while we're journeying here below,
   May this our hopes employ,
That soon in heaven our souls shall know
   A more enduring joy.

Thoughts in solitude

My God! how sweet it is to me
To walk alone and think of thee
     When all around,
       Sight, sense and sound,
Soothe my glad soul to piety.

Ah! would that thus it ever were!
But visions vain my thoughts oft share,
     The wild-fire's gleams,
       And earthly dreams,
That lead to darkness and despair.

Methinks I am a very child,
By each deceit and toy beguiled;
     My Father's breast
       Is now my rest,
And now I court each fancy wild.

O could I always feel and know
That thou alone canst bliss bestow!
     So I might learn
       No more to burn
For transient pleasures here below.

What do I gain? a painted toy!
A fool's delight! a dreaming joy!
     And shall I choose
       For these to lose
Joys which the Christian's heart employ?

O Jesus! grant thou me, I pray,
No more to dream my life away;
    May thy bright grace
    These phantoms chase!
Hold fast my heart, or it will stray.

Thy blessing is on thy people

O grant thy blessing, Lord,
    On all that thou dost give;
May all thou dost afford
    More fit my soul to live;
And thus I shall be doubly blest
And, safe from every danger, rest.

My *daily labours,* bless,
    Or vainly I shall toil,
And, have I more or less,
    Make me content the while;
In vain thy foes shall vigils keep,
But thou wilt give thy loved ones sleep.

O bless the *friends* I love,
    Lord make them seek thy face;
Fix all their hearts above,
    And give them plenteous grace;
O show them, when they count the cost,
By those who hate thee, what is lost.

My Saviour! bless my *soul*
    With light and strength and joy;
My every wish control,
    My every thought employ!
O deign upon my heart to shine,
For thine it is, and only thine!

My *trials* too, my God,
    O'errule them for the best;
And when I've kissed the rod,
    And all my sins confessed,
In thy good time look down I pray,
And take the cause of grief away.

Thou canst e'en bless the last
    Most dreaded of earth's woes;
And, when life's day is past,
    In peace my eyelids close!
O then, – I can desire no more, –
Safe land me on th'eternal shore.

Thy blessing is upon thy people

Thou sayest, Lord, thy blessings are
    On thine own people poured, –
Who are these objects of thy care,
    The people of earth's Lord?

Say, are their names enrolled in heaven?
    On earth are they renowned?
Nay, cease thy search, for God has given
    A rule by which they're found.

A book there is, within is penned
    A transcript of their life;
They learn thereby their ways to mend,
    To shun all sin and strife.

A pattern there they also see
    Of One who came from heaven
To show to sinners such as we
    How they may be forgiven.

And 'tis his people's earnest care
    To tread the path he trod,
The path of duty, love, and prayer,
    That leads direct to God.

Then look around, and when you view
    These tokens of God's own,
Be not thy heart dismayed that few
    Seem in this desert sown.

A little flock, they are, but blest
    With his their Shepherd's smile;
His eyes in love upon them rest; –
    And wait a little while; –

And surely thou shalt see that 'tis
    His own most pleasant thought
To make them heirs of endless bliss,
    For them so dearly bought.

A king shall each be, and a priest,
    To God, and to his Son;
Like stars shall shine the very least,
    Like suns, put glory on.

Then choose thy portion with them now;
    And on that glorious day
A crown of grace shall deck thy brow,
    And joys that ne'er decay.

"To die is gain"

When my conscience is at rest,
When my sins are all confessed,
And I've tried to do my best,
    I do not fear to die.

When I must on things above, –
Heaven's delights, and Jesu's love, –
With desire my bosom move
    To burst life's bands, and die.

But when on my friends I think,
How their hearts with grief would sink!
From the prospect sad I shrink,
    And wish not yet to die.

When life's evils vex my heart,
When from dearest friends I part,
Under grief's sharp wounds I smart,
    And could in spirit die;

In the days when summer showers,
Fair, and rich, sweet fruits and flowers,
And sweet music fills the bowers,
    Then, O my God! I cry:

"If so sweet, and so divine,
These low scenes with glory shine,
What is thine abode, e'en thine,
    Where spring shall never die?"

O! that I those realms could see
Where no sorrow e'er shall be!
Is a mansion there for me?
    O! had I wings to fly;

Might the dove her pinions lend,
Straight I would to heaven ascend!
There are joys that cannot end,
    Where grief shall ne'er come nigh!

Make my soul thy constant care,
Me for life or death prepare;
May I grow more meet to share
    The bliss of saints on high.

Nor may I forget, O Lord,
That, though peace is now restored,
And I, bending to thy word,
    Can say, "now let me die; –"

It hath not been always so;
Once my heart reposed below,
And I sought my will to do,
    Not thine, O God most high!

But, when the enchantment past,
Reason gained her sway at last,
On my deeds her light she cast,
　　O, then I feared to die!

Conscience ope'd her dreadful book,
Bidding me upon it look,
Then on him whom I forsook, –
　　How could I dare to die?

But, Lord, now my sin I leave,
For my former sins I grieve,
And thy willingness believe
　　To hear my contrite sigh.

Bid me now keep near to thee,
Teach me from all ill to flee,
May I ever waiting be,
　　Thy summons, Lord, to die!

Give me every grace I need,
With heaven's bread my spirit feed,
To the living waters lead,
　　And may I daily die!

"Walk by faith, and not by sight"

In every thing you say or do,
Always keep heavenly things in view:
When you to slumber sink at night,
Be death and judgment in your sight;
As you awake at early dawn,
Think of the resurrection morn;
Bathing in water fresh and clean,
Pray to be washed from every sin;
When with your shoes, you clothe your feet,
That God will keep your ways, intreat;
As you your body neatly dress,
Strive to be clothed with holiness;
Before your daily food you eat,
Pray to be fed with heavenly meat;
And when to quench your thirst you drink,
Of Jesus' cup of suffering think;
If you abroad for pleasure walk,
Of peaceful paths of wisdom talk;
The light that warms and cheers your way
Reminds of heaven's far better day;
The sun that shines so clear and bright,
Is type of Christ our life and light;
Your happy home, so safe and warm,
Shows Christ who guards from every harm.
In all then that falls out to you,
Ever keep heavenly things in view;
For wisdom you may gain from all,
However trifling, mean and small;
Then those who little things despise
Are surely very far from wise;
He who contemns what's weak and small
By trifling slips, himself shall fall.

Wisdom's invitation

Youthful travellers, I would know,
Whither in such haste ye go.
"Pleasure's footsteps we attend,
Pleasure is our dearest friend."

Travellers! yet a moment, hold!
Have you never yet been told
What's the end of pleasure's way?
Have you never heard it? say?

"No! we neither know nor care;
All our pleasures harmless are;
Nature 'twas, our conduct bid;
She approved whate'er we did."

Children, listen while I show
Where far purer pleasures flow,
Pleasures that, unfading, last
When life's joys are overpast.

Let me guide you to your Lord,
Peace and gladness he'll afford;
He can all your heart employ,
He will give you boundless joy.

"No, friend, this we will not do;
For if we would go with you
Present pleasure must we leave,
And for all past follies grieve."

You are right, repentance is
Your first step towards happiness;
But endure its wholesome pain,
And you ne'er need grieve again.

'Tis not thus with earthly bliss,
  Changing, vain, and cloying 'tis;
  When its first bright charm is o'er,
  'Tis a paradise no more.

'Tis a bondage, and a chain,
  For the trifling and the vain;
  Low at fashion's feet they bow,
  Would escape, but find not how.

But if pleasure's joys could last
  E'en till furthest age be past,
  You must leave them at death's door,
  Never to regain them more,

Very different from this,
  Is a Christian's happiness;
  This, no diminution knows,
  But, like peaceful rivers, flows.

Death, that ends the worldling's bliss,
  Is the crown and seal of his;
  Death for him no terrors knows,
  'Tis his hoped for, sweet repose.

He, in cheerfulness can live,
  And enjoy what God may give;
  Called to die, without dismay,
  Says – "I'll trust him though he slay".

Children, can ye then refuse
  Happiness so great to choose?
  Ere ye cast such bliss away,
  Think upon my words, I pray.

Turn, and walk in Zion's road,
  Come with us, we'll do you good;
  All our pleasures you shall share,
  We will soothe your every care.

Come! let us together walk,
While of Zion's joys we talk;
There, pure joy and gladness reign,
And we ne'er shall grieve again.

There, when this brief life is o'er,
We may trust to meet once more;
Then, for ever you'll rejoice
That you heard my warning voice.

Children, come, once more I pray,
Dearest! do not say me nay!
Come, and join our pilgrim band,
Hasting toward our native land!

Genesis 22

When God, of Abram, once required
   To slay his only son,
At once he rose as God desired,
   And said, "It shall be done".

But when he says to me, resign
   Thy most beloved sin,
How wilfully do I repine,
   How linger to begin.

And what is it he asks of me?
   How small the sacrifice!
How can so vile an idol be
   So precious in my eyes?

And can I, for a price so small,
   Risk thus my hopes of heaven?
For such a brief delight, lose all
   God's grace to man has given?

I cannot hope, Lord, thou wilt say
   To me – "withhold thine hand,"
Then give me strength thy foe to slay
   Since thus thou dost command,

Psalm 22

My God, my God, in mercy look on me!
Why hast thou left a soul that trusts on thee?
Why thus in vain do I thy aid require?
Why dost thou scorn to grant my heart's desire?
For O my God! to thee by day I cry,
And yet in vain I wait for thy reply;
In the night season, too, I take no rest,
By bitter grief thus cruelly oppressed;
Yet thou art holy! thou wast ever just,
Thou, whom all Israel worship, praise and trust.
Our fathers hoped in thee, on thee relied,
And ever hast thou all their need supplied.
On thee they called in grief, and succour came;
They trusted thee, nor had they cause for shame.
But as for me, I am of men the scorn,
A very worm, vilest of women born,
An outcast, overlooked by all, I lie,
E'en to the human name scarce right have I;
At sight of me, my neighbours shook their head,
They laughed at all my woes, and mocking said,
"He trusted in his God that he would save;
Now let God show if such a wretch he'll have!"
But thou, O Lord, my only hope on earth,
Hast saved and kept me ever since my birth;
Thou wast my hope in childhood's happy day,
When in my mother's tender arms I lay;
Through all my life I have been left to thee,
Nor doubted thou to death my help would be.
Then go not from me now distress is near,
None else have I to help me, guide or cheer.
Like Bashan's bulls, my foes are pressing round;
They close me in, no refuge have I found;
Like hungry lions seek they to destroy,
And all their powers to do me hurt employ.
While thus they vex my soul from day to day,
My feeble body pines with grief away;
Fasting and pain my wearied limbs relax,
My heart is weaker e'en than yielding wax;

My strength is gone, my tongue is parched and dry,
My only hope is that I soon shall die;
Fierce dogs impatiently around me prowl,
Sinners take counsel to entrap my soul;
Mercy, I should in vain from such entreat,
They pierce with sharpest nails my hands and feet;
Through the parched skin my fleshless bones I see,
They stand and gaze in mockery on me.
My very garments for themselves they take,
And for my seamless vesture, lots they make,
Then do not thou remain far from me, Lord,
Thou art my succour, haste and help afford.
Deliver from the sword my fainting soul,
These bloodhounds' power and rage do thou control;
O save me from the ruthless lion's hold,
As thou hast saved thine own in times of old.
Then to the church will I declare thy name,
And 'mid my brethren all thy praise proclaim;
Then will I say aloud, "O praise the Lord,
All ye that know his love and fear his word!
Seek ye his succour in your every need,
All ye his people, Jacob's favoured seed!
O magnify and fear the Lord your rock,
Ye noble stems of Israel's princely stock!
For God hath not despised, nor doth abhor,
The sad condition of the suffering poor;
And when they called, he did not hide his face,
But heard their cry, and shed on them his grace."
Then, in the assembly of the faithful just,
I will declare his praise in whom I trust.
To meet with those who fear him, I delight,
And pay my grateful offerings in their sight.
Nor shall the poor for ever be oppressed,
The day is coming of their joyful rest;
Then shall they freely in abundance eat
The sweetest grapes, the finest of the wheat;
Then shall they seek the Lord, to sing his praise;
Yea, they shall live in peace through endless days.
Then all the dwellers on the earth shall turn,
Mourn for their sins, with love celestial burn;

Yea all the kindreds of each distant land
Shall serve the Lord, and in his temple stand.
For all the nations unto him pertain,
And he, their king and governor shall reign.
The rich that, by his plenteous bounty, live
For all his love their grateful thanks shall give.
All they that sink into the dust of death
Shall kneel to him who gave and took their breath.
For none, but he who made at first the soul,
Can save, or rule it, succour, or control.
And, blessed hope! though I return to dust,
My seed shall serve the Lord among the just;
They shall be called the sons of God most high;
His shall they live, and unto him shall die;
Yea they shall come and bid the world confess
The truth of God, and he their words shall bless,
Until the world, and all that therein is,
Be born anew, be his, and only his.

Psalm 23

Jesus is my faithful pastor,
    He will never let me want;
He, my shepherd kind, and master,
    Food for all my need will grant.

In the pastures green he feeds me;
    By the waters, still and cool,
Into paths of virtue leads me,
    And restores my wandering soul.

Though through death's dark vale I wander,
    Nothing evil need I fear;
On thy constant care I ponder;
    What can harm, and thou so near?

Thou prepar'st my daily table
    Though mad foes my path surround;
Thou art willing, thou art able,
    Make my cup of joy abound!

Do thou still life's blessing lend me,
   All the years I dwell below;
Here on earth may grace attend me,
   Let me still thy mercies know.

But though here below, I never
   Fail thy heavenly love to taste;
Yet, to joys that last for ever,
   Through life's changing scenes I haste.

Psalm 24

Earth and all that therein is,
Is the Lord's, and only his.
All the compass of the earth,
All that thence derive their birth!
For it stands by his decree,
Built upon the raging sea.

Who shall reach that blest abode?
Who ascend the hill of God?
Who may claim the boundless grace,
To behold that holy place?

Even he whose hands are clean,
He whose soul is pure from sin,
He whose heart is set to flee
Every thought of vanity.
He who, from his earliest youth,
Loves the words of simple truth.

Such shall from their Lord receive
Blessings meet for Him to give;
And, from his salvation's God,
Righteousness shall be bestowed.
Thus shall all who seek his face,
Share the God of Jacob's grace.

Lift your heads, ye gates of gold!
Doors of heaven, your leaves unfold!
Lift your hands, eternal gates;
For the king of glory waits.

King of glory! who is he?
Who but Jesus should he be?
Who, but he renowned for might,
He the matchless in the fight?

Portals of the sky unfold!
When your master you behold;
He the king of glory is,
Victory and might are his.

Who then can the conqueror be?
King of glory? who is he?
Who doth such high title claim?
Jesus is his glorious name!
He who these proud titles boasts
Is our King, the Lord of Hosts!

Psalm 25

I lift my soul to thee, O Lord,
My trust is in thy plighted word,
    In thee I hope alone;
O let me not be put to shame!
Thou art the guardian of my fame,
    O deign the trust to own!

O let not those who on thee wait,
But those who thy commandments hate,
    Be shamed before mankind;
To me thy ways of mercy show,
And teach me in those paths to go
    Where I thy presence find.

O lead me in thine every truth,
O guide and teach me in my youth,
   For thou my Saviour art;
On thee, O Lord, I wait each day,
To thee, thou know'st, I nightly pray,
   To thee I give my heart.

Think not, O Lord, on what I've been,
Remember not my youthful sin,
   But call to mind, I pray,
Thy mercies in the day of old,
And let us, Lord, such deeds behold
   In this, the latter day.

Yea, gracious is the Lord, and kind,
Sinners from him shall mercy find,
   He teacheth them aright;
He guideth in his paths the meek,
The mild and gentle doth he seek,
   For such are his delight.

For all his paths are truth and grace
To such as humbly seek his face,
   And keep his holy law;
Then, Lord, have mercy on my sin,
I have a great transgressor been,
   But wish to sin no more.

And great I know is their reward,
Who fear and rightly serve the Lord,
   And break not his command;
He teacheth them himself to please,
He gives them peace, content and ease,
   And plants them in the land.

They shall his secret purpose know;
To them his promise doth he show,
   His covenant of peace;
Then will I ne'er my Lord forget,
My feet he plucketh from the net,
   His mercies never cease.

Turn then, have pity upon me,
In this my sad extremity,
    For I am desolate;
The waves of sorrow o'er me roll,
Grieved and afflicted is my soul;
    Be then thy mercy great.

For my transgression, Lord, I grieve,
O look upon me and forgive
    All I have done amiss;
For many are my foes, and great,
Remorseless are they in their hate,
    My sorrow is their bliss.

Keep, Lord, my soul, I humbly pray,
O let me not be cast away,
    Thou holiest! most just!
Let all thy blessings fall on me,
For long, O God, alone in thee
    Hath been my spirit's trust.

And not unto myself alone
Be this thy love and mercy shown,
    But, Lord, extend thy grace
To all thy church through endless time;
And may they find in every clime,
    Thy throne their meeting place.

Psalm 63

O God! thou art thy people's God,
    Thee early will I seek;
Through pathless deserts have I trod,
    I am distressed and weak.

For thee my spirit is athirst,
    For thee I sigh alone,
Here in the barren land and cursed,
    Whose springs are dried and gone!

Thee have I sought in times of old,
    In paths of truth and love,
That I thy glory might behold,
    Descending from above.

Than life itself, how better far
    To share thy love would be;
Then where thine own beloved are,
    My lips shall sing of thee.

Thus, while thou shalt prolong my days
    Thy Name will I adore,
And lift my hands to shout thy praise,
    And love thee more and more!

When thus, sweet songs, in praise of thee,
    My blissful lips employ,
My soul shall overflowing be
    With richest gifts of joy.

I think on thee, O do I not?
    When in the night I wake.
O say! have I thy name forgot
    When I my couch forsake?

Could I do less? for thou, my King,
    My help and safeguard art!
Then sheltered by thy fostering wing,
    I'll praise thee from my heart!

My helpless, fainting, fearful soul,
    Hangeth, O Lord, on thee!
Thy counsels, all my thoughts control,
    Thy hand upholdeth me!

My foes, who now their skill employ,
    And plot to work me ill,
I know my God, Thou wilt destroy,
    That I may praise thee still!

They shall (for thou hast pledged thy word),
    From greatest to the least,
Fall by thy own avenging sword
    The prowling fox to feast.

For he who on the Lord relies
    Shall glory in his God;
But he who loveth hurtful lies,
    Shall sharply feel his rod.

Psalm 67

Thou, whom thy redeemed adore,
Bless us ever more and more!
To be merciful incline,
Cause thy face on us to shine.
Praise your Lord ye sacred throngs,
Praise to him alone belongs!

Let thy way of peace be shown,
Let thy saving health be known;
Make thy sovereign grace and worth
Heard in every land on earth.
Yea let every clime confess thee!
Yea let all thy people bless thee!

Let the nations gladly sing
To the Lord their mighty King;
Thou shalt judge in every land,
Thou shalt all earth's kings command.
Every nation shall confess thee,
And with all thy saints shall bless thee!

Then the vineyard and the field,
Hill and vale, their strength shall yield;
God shall every curse remove,
God, our own God, whom we love.
He who blessings on us sends,
Fear him, earth's remotest ends!

Psalm 97

The Saviour reigneth! let the earth,
Let all the isles, resound with mirth;
Around him, see the threatening clouds;
His secret purpose, darkness shrouds;
Fair truth and righteousness alone
Are counsellors before his throne,

A fire proceeding from his mouth
Consumes all foes from north to south;
They would not he should reign o'er them,
And justly doth their king condemn:
No foes shall mar his reign of peace,
He maketh wars for ever cease.

The furthest lands his lightnings saw,
Earth's deep foundations shook with awe,
Hills melt like pliant wax away,
In presence of the Lord of day;
The heavens declare his righteousness,
And earth unites his name to bless!

All they who idol gods adore,
Confounded, raise their heads no more.
Ye idols, to the earth low fall,
And worship him as Lord of all!
For Satan from his throne is hurled,
And idols cease in all the world.

Sion shall hear it and rejoice,
Judah's glad daughters lift their voice;
Him praise, they who salvation wrought,
And all their foes to shame hath brought.
The bold oppressor is oppressed,
And saints long suffering now are blest.

Far high exalted, Lord, art thou,
No rival powers oppose thee now,
Thy enemies have felt the rod,
And quailed beneath thy look, O God!
The vials of thy wrath they've drunk,
And far beneath thy scorn are sunk.

And now, all ye that love your Lord,
Revere and always keep his word;
His every known command fulfil,
And hate the appearance e'en of ill;
Your Saviour's eye your path observes,
'Tis He from every ill preserves.

His light to guide your path appears,
And joy divine your spirits cheers.
O then ye righteous, when ye sing,
In honour be it, of your king,
His sacred name adore and bless
In memory of his holiness!

Psalm 106

Give thanks unto the Lord,
His holy name adore;
O sing ye to his praise,
Ye saints, for evermore;
For gracious is our God,
His promises are sure,
His mercy, truth and love,
For ever shall endure!

O who can half recount
Thy noble acts O Lord?
Thy deeds in olden time
'Twere endless to record;
He who to count them o'er
Should dedicate his days
Still would not mention all,
Nor show forth half thy praise!

How blessed is their case
Who, let whate'er betide,
In upright paths of truth
Dare firmly to abide;
Who, scorning crooked ways,
Do what is just and right,
And, while in earth's dark vales,
Keep heaven within their sight.

Theirs be my portion, Lord,
With them may I be blessed!
With them I grieve and toil,
With them, O let me rest!
Remember me O God,
And let me share the grace
Which thou didst shower of old
Upon thy favoured race.

With thy salvation now
O turn and visit me.
The joys of my beloved,
Be mine to share, to see;
And in thy people's good
O give me to rejoice,
Yea with their hallowed songs,
To join my lowly voice!

Yes Lord, though we have sinned,
As all our fathers have,
And oft thy laws transgressed,
O look on us and save!
Preserve and gather us
From those who now oppress,
That we may boast in thee,
That we thy name may bless!

Psalm 107

Ye sons of men! your God and Saviour praise,
Whose endless, boundless mercy crowns your days;
But chiefly let his own redeemed sing,
From all their foes he doth deliverance bring;
He gathereth his elect from every land,
He guides their faltering steps with careful hand;
In desert paths they wandered nigh to hell,
No friendly city found they, where to dwell;
With hunger fainting and with thirst oppressed,
In vain they sought refreshment, food and rest;
Then prayed they to Jehovah in their woes,
He saved them from their sorrows and their foes,
Their wandering feet directed in the way
That leads to regions of eternal day.
O then that men would join their Lord to bless,
His wonders magnify, his love confess!
Who satisfies the longing heart's desires
With every good the waiting soul inspires!

Such as in darkness draw their panting breath,
Bound by the terrors of undying death, –
Why do they thus for bitter bondage sigh?
Because they have contemned the God most high,
Because they would against his words rebel,
And love the flowery ways that lead to hell.
Then God, because he would compassion show,
Gave them the bitter fruits of sin to know;
With deep affliction he brought down their heart,

No friend they found to soothe grief's bitter smart;
At last to God they sought, thus bowed with woes;
He quickly brought their sorrows to a close;
His hand was soon stretched forth to heal and save,
He drew them from the confines of the grave.
O then that all would join our Lord to bless,
His name to magnify, his love confess!
For he the gates of strongest brass hath broke,
And freed us of our chains, our sins, our yoke!

Fools, by their crimes, provoke the wrath of God,
By mad iniquities draw down his rod;
Their food they loathe; they writhe, and gasp for breath;
Each hour they draw more near the gates of death:
Then to the Lord in their despair they cry,
And he to save and heal their soul draws nigh.
He speaks the word and frees them of their grief,
And from destruction sends them sure relief;

Then, O that men would praise their gracious Lord
Who such sweet proofs of mercy doth afford!
O that his name from henceforth they would bless,
His wondrous deeds with gratitude confess!
Yea, let them offer sacrifice of praise,
And altars in their hearts to serve him raise!

They too, whose home is on the restless sea,
Who risk their lives, resistless wealth! for thee;
These, as by day and night, a watch they keep,
Behold thy wonders in the awful deep,
On all around, they see engraved this word,
"We are the works of an Almighty Lord."
E'en in the calm, such lessons they may find;
But, when thou callest forth the stormy wind,
When dreadful waves, as high as mountains, roll,
And the tossed vessel mocks their weak control,
Now low they sink, and now as high arise,
Plunge now beneath the waves, now touch the skies;
Their spirits melt with fear and poignant grief,
And scarce they dream of succour and relief;

Like drunken men, they stagger and they reel,
And, stung to madness, desperation feel;
Then, as a last resource, to God they cry;
He waits to bless; to save them he draws nigh;
He plucks them from their danger and distress,
(He asked but that they should his power confess;)
He stills the waves, he banishes alarm,
And, at his word, nature once more is calm;
Then are they glad, because they are at rest,
He brings them to the haven they love best.
O let them then, their glad Hosannas raise,
And God, for all his tender mercies, praise;
Let them exalt him in his courts below
That all the church his wondrous deeds may know;
Let them exalt him in the Elders' seat,
And bless him wheresoe'er his people meet. –

He turns the waters to a barren plain,
The mountain springs he dries for lack of rain;
The fruitful field he makes a useless spot,
Because his people have his ways forgot.
Again, – he bids the wild with springs abound,
And pours soft streams upon the parched ground,
There he invites the hungering souls to come,
That they may build them a commodious home;
He bids them sow the wheat and plant the vine,
He fills their barn with grain, their vats with wine;

He blesses, and their families increase,
He makes their trials for a time to cease,
And crowns their years with health, content and peace.
Yea, though distressed by treachery and woe,
He makes their tears a little while to flow.
Though forced a tyrant's mandate to obey,
Though far from home, though wandering from the way,
Yet will the Lord exalt his saints on high,
And, like a flock, augment their family;
The good shall see, and in their God rejoice,
Envy, for shame, shall still her odious voice!

Then let the wise on these my words attend,
And seek this God of mercy for their friend.
So on this earth, they shall be richly blessed,
And share in heaven a full and glorious rest.

Psalm 119: 67

We fain would trust thee, – but 'tis not
    Till evil comes indeed,
That we perceive, whate'er our lot,
    How much thy help we need.
Then feel we the command is sweet
To cast our sorrows at thy feet.

We love to pray! – and yet when all
    Around, is calm and fair,
Though on our Maker's name we call,
    How cold is oft our prayer!
But when with grief's sharp wounds we smart,
Prayer springs unbidden from the heart.

We say we on thy word rely;
    Yet who, till want arrives,
Trusts in thee only to supply
    The bread whereby he lives?
Then with what fervour do we say,
"Lord, give us daily bread today!"

We think that Christ is all our stay,
    Our hope but in his blood;
Yet who, until his dying day,
    Leans on him as he should?
But when all life's deceits are past,
O how we cling to him at last!

O! sad, that human hearts should be
    Unbending till they break;
That, till an end of joy they see,
    That joy their god they make.
Then if 'tis so with us, O God!
Is not thy kindest gift thy rod?

But let it, Saviour, not be thus,
   With me and those I love;
O place thy guardian arm round us,
   And draw our hearts above!
But if we will not thus be led,
In grace pour sorrows on our head!

Psalm 120

I called on God when worn with pain.
Who has e'er called on him in vain?
   At least I never have:
I said, "From sinners save my soul,
Their purpose of deceit control.
   And me thy servant save".

What shall in recompense be done
To him who leaseth with his tongue
   And setteth friends at strife?
Mischief shall on his head return,
Half burning coals his heart shall burn,
   And vex him all his life.

Woe, woe is me that I must dwell
'Mid tongues inflamed with strifes of hell,
   Whose quarrels never cease;
In scenes of war I pass my life,
Condemned to witness constant strife,
   Though much I wish for peace.

To end their quarrels oft I seek;
But when on such a theme I speak
   And beg they'll strive no more,
Their anger kindles at my words,
At once they seize their spears and swords,
   And wage more bitter war.

Thus in my grief did I complain,
Nor poured out my soul in vain
   To him who heareth prayer;
He doth my foes' designs control,
He cheers and renovates my soul,
   And strengthens me to bear.

And soon I trust the day will come
That I shall reach my happy home
   Where love and quiet reign;
And when I gain that happy shore,
No foe shall e'er molest me more,
   Nor shall I sigh again.

But while I sojourn here below,
O grant me Lord, thy peace to know,
   My heart on thee I stay;
Give me the peace that passeth thought,
Which Christ with his own blood has bought,
   Peace ne'er to pass away.

Psalm 121

To thee I lift mine eyes,
   From thee my hopes arise,
Whate'er betide, in thee I put my trust;
   In thee, all-powerful Lord,
   Who, by a single word,
Made heaven of nought, and framed this world of dust.

   Guarded by him and loved,
   Thou never shalt be moved,
For God himself a watch shall o'er thee keep:
   In peace let Israel rest,
   By no vain fears oppressed;
God keeps thee, and the Lord doth never sleep!

God is himself thy stay,
He keeps thee night and day,
He is thy sure defence on either hand.
The sun's oppressive light,
The baneful moon by night,
Shall never burn thee, stayed by his command.

He shall thy foes control,
Yea, he shall keep thy soul,
He shall thy steps, where'er thou stray'st, defend;
He shall protect thy head,
And watch around thy bed,
And keep thee safe when life itself shall end.

Psalm 123

To thee I lift my mournful eyes,
O thou who dwell'st beyond the skies.
E'en as a servant's looks will bend
His master's orders to attend,
And as a maiden's eyes enquire
To learn her mistress's desire,
So look we now to thee, O Lord,
Till thou assistance shalt afford.

Have mercy on us, Lord, we pray,
Have mercy! do not now delay;
For men, our confidence despise,
And we are madmen in their eyes;
Our soul is filled with their scorn
Who boast them wealthy, nobly born;
The proud o'erwhelm us with despite,
And our vexed souls are sunk in night!

Psalm 125

They, Lord, who put their trust in thee
Like Sion's sacred mount shall be
Which none can move, it standeth fast,
And ever shall, till time be past.

The hills surround Jerusalem;
Just so the Lord protecteth them.
The wicked's punishments shall ne'er
Be his beloved people's share.

Do well, O gracious God, to all
Who serve thee, and upon thee call;
But they who virtue's path forsake
Shall of the sinners' cup partake;
Thy foes shall all be cast to hell,
But peace shall be to Israel.

Psalm 131

Lord, I'm not to pride inclined,
I am not of haughty mind;
Occupied I will not be
In affairs too high for me.

But my spirit will control,
Chasten and refrain my soul;
Towards my brethren will be mild,
Gentle as a weaned child.

Thus, O Christians, be ye all,
Trust in God, and on him call;
Trust in Christ, his name adore
From this time for evermore.

Psalm 134

O praise ye the Lord! ye his servants, I pray,
Who stand in his temple by night and by day;
E'en ye who enjoy such a sacred abode,
Whose tranquil retreat is the house of your God.

O lift up your hands in that much favoured place,
Lift your hearts and adore the God of all grace;
And blessings from Sion to you shall be given
From Him who created the earth and the heaven.

Psalm 146

Arise my soul thy Lord to praise!
My heart shall bless him all my days;
Yea, when my heart shall cease to beat,
In heaven his praise I will repeat!

O put ye not in kings your trust,
Lean not on any child of dust;
O trust no more in Adam's seed,
Vain is their help in time of need,

Uncertain, fleeting is their breath;
It passes, and they sink in death;
And all the brilliant hopes you cherish
With those who give them birth shall perish

But blest, yes truly blest, are they
Who on the Christian's Saviour stay,
Who do not fear to trust his word,
Whose hope and strength is in the Lord.

He, bountiful, and kind and wise,
Formed the bright earth, the sea, the skies;
And ever faithful to his word,
Food to his creatures doth afford.

He helps the injured to their right
When vexed by godless sinners' might;
And when his people suffer need,
Their souls with goodness doth he feed.

The Lord unlocks the prisoner's chain,
He bids the blind look up again;
Their Maker's help the fallen share,
The righteous are his special care.

Strangers he doth defend and bless,
The widows too, and fatherless;
But the ungodly sinner's path
The Lord shall cross it in his wrath.

O Sion! he whom we adore
Shall be thy king for evermore.
From age to age in thee we'll bless,
Jehovah! God! our Righteousness!

Psalm 150

O bless the glorious author of our days!
Him for his majesty, adore and praise!
Him bless for all his noble acts of power;
Him who in majesty excels, adore!
O praise him in the warlike trumpet's sound;
Praise him where'er the harp and lute are found;
Praise him where'er the joyous dance and sing;
To aid the pomp, soft pipe and cymbal bring:
On cymbals, praise him, well attuned and loud.
Join all ye heathen, to his temple crowd;
Let all things breathing join the sacred mirth,
Yea, fear and praise the Ruler of the earth!

Matthew 6: 19ff

Ye who love pomp and wealth, bend low your ear
Your master's solemn message now to hear;
Ye that are poor, and fear to trust the Lord,
Approach, and listen to his cheering word!
O lay not up! (the heaven-born preacher cries,)
Strive not for treasures found beneath the skies;
Here, moth and rust corrupt your precious stores,
Thieves steal your gold, how strong soe'er your doors;
Here, riches make them wings, and fly away,
The gain of years may vanish in a day;
To you a nobler hope of gain is given,
Safely lay up your treasured stores in heaven!
There, envious rust shall come not near your gold,
There, never entereth in the robber bold!
There, where your treasure is, your heart must be,
Fix it above! there thou shalt reign with me.
With child-like confidence, and heaven-raised eye,
Seek'st thou by prayer to penetrate the sky?
The love of gold will cloud faith's evidence,
And soil thy blood-washed robe of innocence;
'Twill make the very light of life to be
A darkened screen 'twixt heaven's delights and thee.
No man can serve two lords of differing will;
One he must hate, the other's laws fulfil;
Nor can *ye* serve, – whate'er ye hope to do,
The God of heaven and gilded mammon too.
Then hear, all ye who own me for your Lord,
Hear ye my promise, hear my warning word!
O be not anxious for tomorrow's bread,
Sure shall your waters be, ye shall be fed!
Ask not, what clothes your shivering limbs shall wear,
For all your wants are God's especial care.
He gives you life, and shall he not provide
Food to supply life's fluctuating tide?
He made your body; can you then suppose
He will forget that body needeth clothes?
Behold! and all these fears before you chase,
Look, and learn wisdom from the feathered race;

They sow not in the spring, nor do they reap;
No granaries to hold their store, they keep,
And yet your Father doth the ravens feed!
And can you think he will forget your need?
Who, by deep thought, could to his stature add?
Then are ye anxious how ye shall be clad?
Look at yon glorious lilies as they grow!
They spin not – labour's toils they cannot know,
Yet Solomon in all his pomp and might,
Was not arrayed in garments half so bright.
Then if God clotheth thus the short- lived flower,
Cast in the oven, ere it bloom an hour,
Shall he not much more clothe each trembling limb
Of all his children who will trust in him?
Take then no thought, – O! do not ever say,
What shall we do in life's declining day?
What shall we eat, or drink? or wherewithal
Shall there be raiment to array us all?
For, God himself, your need, your weakness knows,
They cannot want who on his word repose;
He says, "seek first heaven's grace and righteousness,
God all things addeth, and your souls will bless!"
Be then your lives exempt from care and sorrow,
Leave in God's hands provision for the morrow.

Matthew 10: 37

He that loveth friend or brother,
He that father loves or mother,
Better than he loveth me,
Cannot my disciple be.

He who dotes upon himself,
On his pleasures, lands, or pelf,
Whatsoe'er his idol be,
Cannot hope to live with me.

He who, – Zion's road begun, –
Turns before his race is run,
Need not hope my son to be;
He is quite unworthy me.

He who boasts celestial birth
While his heart is all on earth,
Ne'er shall my salvation see;
Fool for every world is he.

I from such, will turn away,
Though "O Lord we're thine," they say;
None can my disciple be
Who gives not his life to me.

Lord I yield thee then my heart,
Reign there, order every part;
Nothing would I do or be
Other than resigned to thee.

Nothing would I seek or love.
What should my ambition move?
Whom in heaven have I but thee?
Be thou all on earth to me!

Make me Lord for ever thine!
Be thou still kind Saviour, mine!
Here on earth I thine will be,
Let me thy salvation see!

Luke 6

As still and wakeful, on my couch I lie,
What lovely vision fills my fancy's eye?
As day declines, and all is hushed and still,
Who climbs the brow of yonder lofty hill?
Dost thou not recognize that face divine
Where all the Godhead's rays attempered shine?
Such loveliness as artist ne'er could paint,

Meekness more lowly than of martyred saint!
Such dignity as kings assume in vain,
Beseeming *him* long wont o'er kings to reign; –
What self-devotion beams in every look!
'Tis he who for lost man heaven's throne forsook!
(What love to God! what boundless love to men,
Shone in his heavenly features even then!
But what his beauty, could we see him now,
When crowns of vict'ry decorate his brow! –
Where high archangels low before him fall,
And saints adore *Him* who redeemed them all;
Where far in glory he excels the sun; –
There reigned he glorious ere had time begun,
There shall he reign, when time its course has run;
He thence descended only for man's sake,
Our nature took, that we might his partake.)
But see! he now hath scaled the mountain high.
Behold his lifted hands! his kindling eye!
The sun, departing, leaves him wrapt in prayer,
The rising sun, finds him still kneeling there,
What is his prayer? – needs *he* a Father's grace,
Whose heart is perfect virtue's dwelling place?
Or is it for the friends he left below
That his petitions thus unwearied flow?
Yes, doubtless; all his wrestlings, tears and prayers,
Were not for his advantage, but for theirs;
Those whom by day so earnestly he taught,
On them by night heaven's blessings he besought,
All methods for their good the Lord essayed;
He laboured wisely, – earnestly he prayed;
Yet not to them alone his cares extend,
But all his church till time itself shall end;
Not to those only who *then* called him Lord,
But future converts who should hear their word.
Perhaps, my soul! then e'en for thee he prayed,
In thy behalf were those petitions made;
O! may thou never lose, for lack of care,
The blessings gained thee by thy Saviour's prayer!
Entreat him, he that taught thee how to pray,
To grant thee all the gifts he asked that day!

But, now that morn returns, to meet his friends,
And waiting followers, the Lord descends:
His heavenly converse quits at duty's call;
Not to himself he lives, – he lives for all:
Inspired by heaven, of twelve he makes his choice
From those long guided by their Shepherd's voice,
Who should, when he was gone, those precepts teach,
'Twas now the business of his life to preach.
Met, and attended, by this favoured train,
The Lord descends, and hastens to the plain;
There, wondering multitudes impatient stand,
To view the marvels wrought at his command;
The blind, the deaf, the halt, the maimed, come,
And healed by him, return rejoicing home.
He grants each suppliant every grace he needs,
The dead he raises, and the hungering feeds.
Then, on his own beloved his eyes he turns,
While inspiration in his accents burns,
And with a father's zeal, a brother's love,
He thus directs their thoughts to things above;
"Ye poor in spirit! bless'd indeed are ye,
The heirs of God's own kingdom shall ye be,
Bless'd are ye, though ye hunger now, and want;
Wealth plenteous to supply your need he'll grant;
And bless'd are ye that pine in sorrow now!
Eternal mirth shall sit upon your brow;
Yea happy are ye! though the proud contemn,
And count you company unmeet for them;
When, to revile you, they their wit employ;
Rejoice ye, in that day, and leap for joy!
A few brief years, and all your sorrow ends;
One day in heaven shall make you full amends.
Thus, with their fathers, did the prophets fare,
And you like them, are heaven's peculiar care.
But woe to you, ye rich! for you I fear,
Lest heaven you barter for enjoyments here;
And woe to you that now are full! for ye
An end to all your feasting soon shall see.
Woe! woe! to you that now rejoice and sing,
Who, thoughts of God, and death, behind you fling;

And, woe! when all men join to speak your praise;
So did they to false seers, in ancient days.
But you, my friends, your portion is above;
Then imitate your God's extensive love,
Ne'er let earth's follies steal your heart again,
But love as brethren all your fellow men.
Do they provoke, and seek to work you ill?
Be your revenge, forbearance and good will.
Say, do they curse you, injure and oppress?
Return them good, pray for them too, and bless!
To him who asks assistance, freely give;
And lend, where you can nought again receive;
Your liberality shall God repay
A thousand fold, for all you give away.
You, his own children the most high shall call,
Who freely sheds his blessings upon all;
Not only to good he favours gives;
The thankless sinner, by his bounty, lives;
Take then example by your Lord above,
And shed around you benefits and love.
Judge not, and God in judgment shall spare you,
Forgive, and you shall be forgiven too;
For with the measure ye to man accord
Your actions shall be measured by your Lord.
Weigh, ye that teach, these sayings in your mind,
Nor, blind yourselves, attempt to lead the blind.
You pluck the mote from out your brother's eye,
And do your own defects unheeded lie.
If you successfully would cure his sin,
Correct your own worse failings to begin.
Not precepts, e'en the wisest, most divine,
So forcibly, man's heart to good incline,
As does example, pure, consistent, meek,
Proving, yourselves believe the words you speak.
Begin then with your hearts; these, probe and know,
How can great actions from vile motives flow?
For every tree is by its fruit discerned;
If barren, soon it is cut down and burned;
Is the tree good? then good its fruits will be,
But evil fruits denote a worthless tree:

Can thorns, the sweet and luscious fig produce?
Or brambles yield the grape's reviving juice?
Let no man dare my sacred laws to preach
Whose deeds belie what he presumes to teach.
Why tempt ye me, by calling me "Lord! Lord!"
Unless as subjects ye obey my word?
– The man who comes to me, and bends his ear
To practise every duty he shall hear,
That man, to a wise builder I compare,
Who, ere he builds, selects a site with care,
Erects his tower on the unyielding rock,
And firmly it sustains the tempest's shock;
Though floods arise, though madly howls the storm,
He fears it not, within his shelter warm;
Against it rush the torrents madly, still,
But cannot shake the everlasting hill.
But *he*, vain sinner! who his duty learns,
And yet from wisdom's paths his footsteps turns,
Him will I liken to the thoughtless man
Who rears his house in haste, without a plan,
Who builds upon the earth by flowery streams,
But loss of time to dig below he deems:
While summer's days endure, and cloudless skies,
His lofty turrets, fair and towering rise;
Though summer's calms are quickly gone and past,
He builds, as if they would for ever last.
But winter comes – he gazes with surprise,
On raging floods, and darkly threatening skies,
Begins to fear his former plans were wrong,
But, nor his fears, nor doubts, continue long;
The first high flood his frail embankment breaks,
His gay built towers the raging tempest shakes,
One moment more, and all his buildings fall,
The next wave sweeps away himself and all."
He said, who spake as man ne'er spake before,
These memorable words, nor added more;
He said, – and, blessing all his listening train,
To proud Capernaum bent his steps again.
Meanwhile – the wondering hearers overawed,
Entranced with joy, had hung on every word;

Some home returning, told to all they met
Those heavenly precepts they would ne'er forget!
While some, alas! as they had heard them not,
Passed lightly by, and soon the whole forgot.
Some hid them in their hearts, whence shone there
    forth
Fair deeds and heavenly words of matchless worth.
And *one* there was, who did, *nor* light depart,–
Nor only hid the words within his heart;
That man, the pen of the instructed took,
And wrote the heavenly sermon in a book.
Thanks "loved physician" for thy well used lore,
Thy scroll, the more I read, I prize it more!
O envied man! who from the fountain's head
Drank living streams! – on heavenly manna, fed,
E'en when his master from his sight was gone,
He was not in life's desert left alone,
A friend he found, who the same Lord obeyed;
At once they taught, they journeyed and they prayed;
When parted, what but union was their prayer,
Their joys were one, their hopes, their every care.
O envied Silas! to be thus beloved,
Of him whom death, nor stripes, nor dungeon moved,
Of him, the champion of the Christian cause,
Who through the world proclaimed his master's laws;
What saint in heaven so high advanced as Paul,
Who laboured more abundantly than all!
Or if humility gain honour's post,
'Tis his – though few have had such cause to boast!
But hold! while musing time flies swiftly hence,
Thy spirit, slumber, steals each weary sense.
Adieu ye thoughts, pleasing as flowers of May,
Adieu, – but O! return at dawn of day;
And thou my soul, ere thou to slumber sink,
With thankfulness on all past mercies think.
To God most high I now that soul commend;
Sweet dreams, and tranquil slumbers may he send:

And waking, may I still those truths revere
Which musing on my couch, my spirits cheer;
Ne'er may I, from their guidance sweet depart,
But write them on the tablets of my heart.

II Corinthians 5: 8

O how I wish the hour were come
When Christ shall send and fetch me home!
O how my spirit pants and sighs
To join the saved beyond the skies!

My fancy paints the happy throng,
I bend my ear to catch their song;
I envy them their robes so white,
Their palms so green, and crowns so bright.

Their woes, their fears, their pains are o'er,
Sin never shall distress them more,
No more oppressed and faint, they toil,
No more their blood-washed raiment soil.

O bless'd! they see their Saviour's face,
They feel the Spirit's boundless grace,
Unnumbered beauties charm their eyes,
They eat the fruits of Paradise.

Admit me soon, Lord, I entreat,
To share a life so pure and sweet,
O fit me for it soon, I pray,
Then haste and call my soul away!

Galatians 3: 9

O give a right faith, dearest Saviour, to me!
A faith, that for righteousness counted, may be;
Like Abram, the father of all that believe,
Thy promise confidingly, may I receive,

"Arise!" saith thy word on my conscience impressed,
"The sin which thou lovest, root out of thy breast.
Arise! from things earthly deliver thy heart;
Prepare! to a land I will show thee, depart!

The things thou best lovest, whenever I call,
Be ready, for my sake, to offer them all;
Go where I appoint thee, be faithful to me,
And, as I bless'd Abraham, will I bless thee."

That thus I may serve Thee, O give me the will,
Then add, Lord, the power such desires to fulfil.
Be my life like his, and at last may I rest,
With all his true children, on Abraham's breast!

I Timothy 2: 1

Lord thy word hath plainly spoken,
  Men for each other pray;
This I hail a joyful token,
  Thou wilt hear the words I say;
    At thy command,
    I praying stand,
To beg thy favour for my native land.

Ever were we, Lord, a nation,
  Blessed by thy peculiar care,
Safe in midst of desolation,
  Peaceful while around was war,
    Sealed from the wrath,
    Thou pouredst forth,
On every neighbouring land from south to north.

In the troubles now impending,
  Do as thou hast ever done,
If thou plagues on earth art sending,
  If e'en now thou hast begun,
    This country spare,
    Once more forbear,
For their sakes who thy faithful servants are.

Though our sins be very grievous,
  Though the people madly rage,
Be thou not provoked to leave us,
  Thou our help from age to age;
    Grant still thy grace
    A little space,
And do not from our troubles hide thy face.

If the day so long predicted
  Now is hasting to its dawn,
When thy church so long afflicted,
  Shall no more by strife be torn,
    Now at the last,
    O! do not cast,
From thee the land beloved in ages past.

May our country be a Zoar,
  Spare us for the righteous' sake;
Or, as in the days of Noah,
  For thy church a refuge make!
    Yet, Lord, thy will
    In all fulfil,
And may we each bend to it, and be still!

Notes on Collects

COMPARISON WITH COLLECTS IN 1662 PRAYER BOOK

It will be helpful if the reader compares the following Collects taken from the Book of Common Prayer of 1662 with their versified equivalents in Emily's Hymns and Sacred Poems.

Collect for Quinquagesima Sunday

O Lord, who hast taught us that all our doings without charity are nothing worth; Send thy Holy Ghost, and pour into our hearts that most excellent gift of charity, the very bond of peace and of all virtues, without which whosoever liveth is counted dead before thee: Grant this for thine only Son Jesus Christ's sake, Amen.

Collect for the First Sunday in Advent

Almighty God, give us grace that we may cast away the works of darkness, and put upon us the armour of light, now in the time of this mortal life, in which thy Son Jesus Christ came to visit us in great humility; that in the last day, when he shall come again in his glorious majesty to judge both the quick and the dead, we may rise to the life immortal, through him that liveth and reigneth with the Holy Ghost, now and ever, Amen.

Collect for the Second Sunday in Advent

Blessed Lord, who hast caused all holy Scriptures to be written for our learning; Grant that we may in such wise hear them, read, mark, learn, and inwardly digest them, that by patience and comfort of thy holy Word, we may embrace and ever hold fast the blessed hope of everlasting life which thou hast given us in our Saviour Jesus Christ, Amen.

Collect for the Fourth Sunday in Advent

O Lord, raise up, we pray thee, thy power, and come among us, and with great might succour us, that whereas, through our sins and wickedness, we are sore let and hindered in running the race that is set before us, thy bountiful grace and mercy may speedily help and deliver us; through the satisfaction of thy Son our Lord, to whom with thee and the Holy Ghost be honour and glory, world without end, Amen.

Collect for the 21st Sunday after Trinity

Grant, we beseech thee, merciful Lord, to thy faithful people pardon and peace, that they may be cleansed from all their sins, and serve thee with a quiet mind, through Jesus Christ our Lord, Amen.

GENERAL INDEX

INDEX OF FIRST LINES OF HYMNS AND POEMS